AFRICA—HOPE DEFERRED

AFRICA—
HOPE DEFERRED

JOHN BIGGS-DAVISON M.P.

JOHNSON
LONDON

JOHN BIGGS-DAVISON © 1972

First Published 1972

ISBN 0 85307 090 3

SET IN 11 ON 12 PT BASKERVILLE AND PRINTED BY
CLARKE, DOBLE & BRENDON LTD., PLYMOUTH.
FOR JOHNSON PUBLICATIONS LTD.,
11/14 STANHOPE MEWS WEST, LONDON, S.W.7

CONTENTS

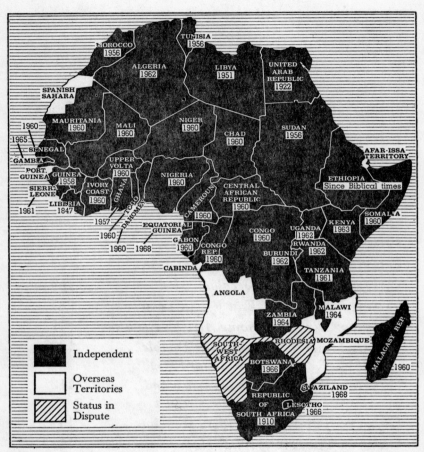

By Henry Benson, staff cartographer

With acknowledgements to the 'Christian Science Monitor'

THE NEW AFRICA

CHAPTER I

Black versus Black

From the village of Nhica do Rovuma on the Portuguese
side of the river which separates Mozambique from Tanzania, one can see the smoke of cooking fires rising from
the far bank. It seems peaceful enough but the villagers of
Nhica are not deceived. They man bunkers and crude
watch towers, expectant of the next attack. Once, a third
of the village was destroyed by enemy mortars, but the
villagers can point with pride to an arsenal of captured
enemy weapons. Life, then, is organised on military lines.
Armed patrols scour the bush and accompany the women
into the fields to harvest the maize crop. Back in the village
a solitary Portuguese policeman directs the defences. The
near-naked children grow up knowing nothing but a state
of war.

The villagers of Nhica are black. Their attackers from
across the Rovuma are black. All are members of the
Makonde tribe—the Makonde of scarred faces, with a reputation in battle and a delicate and imaginative skill as
carvers of heavy ebony wood. To the Makonde who steal
across the Rovuma to bombard Nhica, the war is one of
"liberation". To the Makonde of Nhica the enemy come not
as liberators but as *turras* (terrorists). Occasionally a Portuguese army patrol will stop at Nhica for a few hours' rest,
or aircraft will land at the nearby strip with supplies of
arms and ammunition; but the war here is mainly fought
by native against native, and there are many Nhicas in the

remote north of Mozambique—many, too, in the vast Portuguese territory of Angola to the west, and in the steamy enclave of Portuguese Guinea, far to the north.

This is the size of the struggle for Southern Africa. It stretches across the southern third of the continent from the mouth of the Congo river to where the Rovuma meets the Indian Ocean. It blazes or smoulders along Angola's border with the Democratic Republic of the Congo; it filters into South-West Africa and flickers spasmodically in Rhodesia's Zambesi valley. From Zambia it infects the district of Tete in Mozambique, whose border with Tanzania is the most hostile of them all.

As the last European power to hold vast territories in sub-Saharan Africa, Portugal bears the main military burden. Since 1961 the Portuguese have fought to defend Angola; since 1963, Guiné; and, since 1964, Mozambique. Portuguese military strength in Africa was raised to 130,000 men in 1970, when the Prime Minister, Dr. Marcello Caetano, committed to the struggle six more regular battalions. This very considerable military effort accounts for 42 per cent of the Portuguese budget.

Portugal is pledged to fight a defensive war within her national boundaries, but those who seek to drive her from Africa have no such inhibitions. They operate from behind frontiers which have so far remained inviolate. They train at camps, hidden in the southern parts of Tanzania—at Mbeya, Nachingwea, Masasi, Tunduru and Mtwara, to name some of the most important. After initial training, self-styled liberation forces are sent on missions across the Rovuma to raid Mozambique, or to transit camps in Zambia; whence the fight can be carried into the heartland of Rhodesia, South-West Africa, or the barren bushland of Eastern Angola. The raiders are armed with the latest

8

weapons from Poland or Peking, often superior to those of their enemies and openly imported through the ports of Mtwara and Dar-es-Salaam, together with Cuban and Chinese instructors.

Tanzania is thus the pivot of the guerrilla movements fighting in Southern Africa. Dar-es-Salaam (which means "haven of peace") is their most important supply centre; and from there the diplomatic and propaganda war is waged against the South. Here are found the offices of FRELIMO,[1] the M.P.L.A.,[1] Z.A.P.U.[1] and Z.A.N.U.[1] of Rhodesia, and the P.A.C.[1] and A.N.C.[1] of South Africa. All these organisations eye each other closely and with suspicion. The two Rhodesian movements only tried to achieve unity in opposition to the Smith government in the winter of 1970. The South African movements are not on speaking terms, while the M.P.L.A. even fight against Holden Roberto's National Front for the Liberation of Angola (F.N.L.A.) in that country's dense northern forests. Breakaway groups not recognised by the Organisation of African Unity—such as U.N.I.T.A.[1] of Angola and C.O.R.E.M.O.[1] of Mozambique—attempt to sabotage the efforts of their better-known rivals.

These divisions are exploited by the Portuguese, Rhodesians and South Africans, and so far even the more effective "liberation" movements have met with little success in the field. Portuguese Guinea might be considered indefensible; even so, with most of their troops committed elsewhere, the Portuguese have held this territory the size of Wales in the face of the best equipped liberation army in

[1] Mozambique Liberation Front: Angola People's Liberation Movement: Zimbabwe African People's Union: Zimbabwe African National Union: People's African Congress: African National Congress: National Union for the Total Independence of Angola: Mozambique Revolutionary Committee.

Africa. In Angola, terrorist activity in the north takes the form of hit-and-run raids, with more "scoot" than "shoot"; in the east, the occasional minor disruption of the Benguela Railway hurts the Zambians themselves more than the Portuguese. The war in Mozambique, where there was initial guerrilla success, settled into stalemate in 1970.

Most conspicuous, however, has been the failure of the freedom movements to win what is known in the jargon of counter-intelligence as the hearts and minds struggle. In Guiné, Angola and Mozambique, the Portuguese arm Africans to take part in their own defence—as the villagers of Nhica can confirm. In the Zambesi valley, African villagers have never failed to report terrorist infiltration to the Rhodesian authorities. Whatever the reason for this loyalty, it is a fact, and while it exists, boasts by the revolutionary parties to control some square miles of "liberated" bush are meaningless.

That there would be no terrorist threat without the assistance of countries like Tanzania, which provide the necessary bases, is a fact admitted by the freedom fighters themselves. President Nyerere is an uncompromising opponent of the white south. His natural ally, President Kaunda of Zambia, is in a more difficult position. Despite the xenophobic atmosphere of his country, he must reckon with the economic consequences of Rhodesia's Unilateral Declaration of Independence.

Although South African trade largely covers Rhodesian losses, the Zambian economy relies on the Portuguese railway to the Atlantic at Benguela and to the Indian Ocean at Beira. President Kaunda must therefore contend with the hot-heads within his own government, who would endanger Zambia's fragile prosperity by such demonstrations against Portugal as raids on the Benguela Railway. He thus finds himself compelled to play one side off against the other, excusing the use of his country as a staging post for raids on Angola by the weakness of Zambia's small regular defence force.

The President's attitude to Rhodesia is also ambivalent. Certain commodities must pass between the two countries, if Zambia's mines and factories are to be kept working. Even the Rhodesia railway would cease to function without the efforts of Rhodesian engineers. So Zambia is forced to trade with a rebel state against which most of the world is supposedly at economic war.

Fearful of being outbidden on the Left, and of the danger to the Copperbelt from racial hostility to the European miners, President Kaunda saw in the projected Tan-Zam railway a way of escape from his dilemma. If "the West" declined to build it, why not Peking, whose revolutionary zeal President Nyerere so greatly admires? The formal contract for the railway was signed in 1970. The estimated cost is £167 millions.

Even before this opportunity occurred in Tanzania, Peking had changed its revolutionary strategy in Africa. After the great tour of Arab and African states by the Prime Minister, Chou En-lai, in 1963, Chinese fortunes had undergone vicissitudes. Peking's ideological and commercial offensive suffered setback when its support of rebellion led to the expulsion of its Embassy staff from Bujumbura (Burundi) in 1965 and the second Afro-Asian Conference which it had intended to register the formation of a major Third World bloc under Chinese domination collapsed owing to revolution in Algiers.

At the beginning of 1966 a series of military *coups* in West Africa brought about the expulsion of Chinese diplomatists, technicians and journalists from Dahomey, the Central African Republic and Ghana. Peking's Embassy in Tunisia was closed in 1967. Communist Chinese activities in Africa were further curtailed by the onset of the Cultural Revolution. Its excesses alienated Kenya and relations between the Chinese People's Republic and the para-Marxist régime in Congo-Brazzaville also declined.

In Malawi Peking lost face when President Hastings Banda accepted aid from the Nationalist Chinese government in Taiwan. It then decided to offer aid only to those countries which showed ideological promise or could not afford to refuse it. Their Soviet competitors lost ground as a consequence of the invasion of Czechoslovakia in 1968, and the Chinese Communists increased their aid, supplying both arms and instructors to the guerrilla training camps in Tanzania.

The defenders of Nhica may thus expect a more efficient terrorism and an intensified war against the south. If pressed too far, however, the *méchant animal* of the French saying might defend himself by hitting back as the Israelis did in a similar situation, and such retaliation can be fully justified in international law. No black African movement is as formidable as an *Al-Fatah*, and, as Dr. Banda has said more than once, no black army could openly challenge South Africa, Portugal and Rhodesia in the field.

The Middle East, moreover, has witnessed the dangers which revolutionary guerrilla groups can present to the governments which give them hospitality. President Sekou Touré is no King Hussain, but he may reflect that the forces of the P.A.I.G.C.[2] are stronger than those of the Republic of Guinea which harbours them, and what happened in

[2] African Party for the Independence of Guiné-Bissau and Cape Verde.

Jordan during the winter of 1970 shows how difficult it is
to keep such movements to heel.

Attitudes in the new African states are changing.
Economic and other domestic problems, above all those of
tribalism, increasingly command the full attention of their
rulers. To Chad or the Sudan, those less publicised "Biafras",
the southern freedom struggle seems very far away. The
Organisation for African Unity has its headquarters in
Addis Ababa, but the Lion of Judah must reckon with
the Muslims of Eritrea.

Many other African leaders pay lip service to the aims
and ideals of the Organisation's Liberation Committee, and
keep their hands firmly in their pockets. Slogans denounc-
ing the white states of Southern Africa may serve to cloak
deficiencies in administration and to unite rival tribes; resolutions in the United Nations give an illusion of action
against racialism. But Africa's ills cannot be forever attributed to the white man. As President Nyerere himself has
asked, what would have been the reaction if 30,000 Africans
had been murdered, as in Nigeria, by Rhodesians or South
Africans, rather than by their own "kith and kin"? The
final toll of Nigerian lives is probably in millions. The most
destructive colonial war in African history was not waged
by white against black, but black against black.

The internal weaknesses of the independent African states
will not be remedied by rhetorical calls for revolution in
the south. Revolution is more likely to erupt nearer home
and, as most of Africa's leaders know well, those external
forces which hope for chaos in Southern Africa are eager
and willing to foment it. Furthermore, the example of
Rhodesia has shown beyond a doubt that outside inter-
ference in Southern Africa hardens resistance to any "wind
of change". Africa as a whole may have more cause for

gratitude to rulers who reject Pan-African gestures, and seek trade and intercourse with South Africa, than to the quarrelsome revolutionaries of Dar-es-Salaam.

Change is afoot in South Africa too. The non-European races are playing a more and more prominent part in their country's prosperity, and many Afrikaners have abandoned their traditional agricultural pursuits and have taken to industry and finance. The shortage of skilled labour is more likely to lead to a modification of racial policy than are international boycotts and attempted revolutions. The outward looking foreign policy makes sense to young South Africans studying and touring abroad.

South Africa's toleration is however a sensitive plant, and its growth is retarded by the efforts, sincere or sinister, of the international spoilsport movement and those who have tried to impose their own cultural *apartheid* upon the Republic. Not long ago, a touring team from Pretoria University visited Britain. One of its matches was played against a team which fielded a black player from Sierra Leone, the latter having withstood pressure not to play against a "racialist" side. After the game, the Sierra Leonean attended a reception for the two teams with his wife, who is as white as he is black. At the end of the evening, one young South African said: "For the first time in my life I have spoken to an African on the same level." In June 1970 whites were defeating blacks in the first multi-racial Rugby match at the University of Natal and the blacks were calling for revenge at Soccer.

Let the new states of Southern Africa open their doors to the South Africans, to the Rhodesians and to the Portuguese. Let them demonstrate that black governments can rule justly, that white can be governed by black without fear and intolerance. Conversely, let the independent countries draw on European skill and experience. Malawi under the firm, wise rule of Dr. Hastings Banda, has lost none of her spirit of independence by entering into full diplomatic relations with Pretoria. Nor is Malawi the only independent African state to do business with South Africa and to adopt the policy recommended by an Opposition Member of Parliament at the Cape of association not isolation.

Much that is admirable has been achieved in newly-independent Africa, often on the flimsiest foundations. One thinks of the astonishing economic recovery of the ex-Belgian Congo under President Mobutu, President Kenyatta's unexpectedly enlightened rule in Kenya, the redemption of Ghana from its self-appointed "Redeemer", and the statesmanship of several French-speaking African leaders.

But in many parts of the continent the exalted hopes of Independence Day have been at least deferred. May these pages help to clarify discussion, clear the atmosphere of double talk, double think and double standards, and show that all the tribes and races of many shades of skin who have made their homes in Africa through the centuries of conquest, commerce and migration have a common interest in survival and advancement, and therefore in co-operation.

CHAPTER II

Fact and Fiction

African history is an uncertain study. Reliable documentation is scarce and, much of what passes for history is mere propaganda. The historian Basil Davidson, writing in *The African Past*[1] of two ages of historical importance, is forced to admit that medieval Swahili documents are never discovered—either because Swahili was not yet a written language, or, more probably, because they have vanished forever. Again :

> "There is every reason to believe that learned men in the Empire of Mali, and just possibly of the last phases of the Empire of Ghana, wrote about their beliefs and their conditions; no such works, unhappily, have come down to us."

Thus, the history of Africa lends itself to historical distortion. On the one hand, a superficial "white settler" school of thought insists that, until the arrival of the first Europeans, the Dark Continent lay in Stygian gloom. The twelfth century stone walls of Rhodesia's Zimbabwe, they argue, must have been built by Arab traders; Bantu could never have accomplished such a task. Why, they never invented the wheel !

Alternatively, and no less inaccurately, Marxist and para-Marxist historians attempt to prove the opposite case. Addressing the Atlantic Conference in 1959, Professor Hugh Seton-Watson declared that :

[1] Davidson, Basil: *The African Past* (Penguin).

16

"the creation of the systematic body of doctrine about early historical civilisations in Africa, whether mythical or scientific, is undoubtedly a task assigned to Soviet academic experts on Africa."

Lecturing in Moscow in the same year, the late Professor Ivan Potemkin spoke of restoring "the historical truths about the African people". What he meant was the rewriting of African history in Marxist-Leninist terms. Such a fact was tacitly admitted by the assistant director of the Soviet Africa Institute, Irina Yastrebova, who, in an article published in 1963, wrote of the :

"study (of) the specific features of the working class and peasant movements. We are interested in the role of the working class in the struggle for development, the formation of the alliance of the working class and peasantry as the basis of a national democracy."

The Marxist-Leninist school of African history encouraged the belief of such men as Kwame Nkrumah that they are the heirs of ancient civilisations far excelling those of classical Greece or ancient Rome. Achmed Rechedi's film *L'Aube des Damnés*, shown in July, 1969 at the first Pan-African Cultural Festival, held in Algiers, derided "the baboons of ancient Greece who plagiarised our African culture".

Such historical distortions and extravagances inflate the self-esteem of black nationalist leaders, and nourish the morale of their militant followers, by rubbing the European nose in the dirt of colonial and neo-colonial guilt. Such an indictment is accepted without question by the "progressive" intelligentsia of the West. Jean-Paul Sartre sees Europe's only achievement as cruelty and crime :

"You know well we are exploiters. You know too that we have laid hands on first the gold and the metals, then the

17

petroleum of the new continents and that we have brought
them back to the old countries . . . with us, to be a man is
to be an accomplice of colonialism, since all of us, without
exception, have profited by colonial exploitation."[2]

Such hatred of the colonial past soon matures into a hatred
of Europe herself, an extension of that self-induced guilt complex which is encouraged by those who systematically seek
to undermine the influence of the West in Africa.

What is the truth? In a short study such as this, it is necessary to compress and generalise; all we can attempt to do
is give a general picture. As Roland Oliver asked:

"Is it the Africa of unmitigated savagery, complete with
cannibalism, witchdoctors and poison darts. . . ? Or is it the
ancient Africa of the modern nationalist's dream—rich,
learned, colourful, ceremonious, fun?"[3]

But to generalise about Africa is far more difficult than to
generalise about Europe or the Americas. The nomadic
Masai of Kenya is as different from the Yoruba townsman
in Nigeria, as is a Matabele from a Bulawayo Rotarian. The
Kabyle of Algeria and the Hottentot of South Africa have
less in common than the German and the Greek.

Mokwungo Okoye, the author of *African Responses* and
The Beard of Prometheus, sees in Africa "a great tradition
of personal freedom which is the very antithesis of the
current totalitarian trends in some of her countries". The
ancient African communes resembled the city-states of
ancient Greece. Okoye asserts that the term "chief" was
alien to Africa, and that the despotism discovered by Europeans was a later development. Kingship and chieftancy
were constitutionally limited by the powers enjoyed by
councils of relatives and confidants, and by broader-based

[2] Preface to *Les Damnés de la Terre* by Franz Fanon.
[3] Oliver, Roland: *The Dawn of African History*, O.U.P. 1968

assemblies, composed of lesser chiefs and clan heads. The democratic elements in these "mixed" constitutions led to the development of tribal societies regulated by loyalty, ritual and religion, in which individualism was virtually unknown.

In the Dark Ages, many African Negroes may have lived more easily in their beehive huts than many a villein in Northern Europe. Mokwungo Okoye calls it "a free-for-all society where gods, kings and men commingled in harmonious companionship and each respected the rights of others".[4] African music, assimilated in American melody, served a real social purpose, expressing as it did, the African capacity for joy and harmony. African poetry, too, looks to the past as its golden age.

In those days Europe and Africa seemed to run a parallel course. Later, Africa seemed to stagnate, while Europe thrust ahead. The Negro, until the arrival of foreign invaders, wandered and hunted, tilled and worshipped in ancestral fashion. Without draft beasts, carts or wheels, he advanced little or not at all in agricultural efficiency. Whereas beside the Mediterranean the swing plough was used, south of the Saharan wilderness the hoe did duty. When the Arab caravans crossed the desert to the Niger or to Senegal, they brought with them no technological revolution, but trade goods—baubles and trinkets, tobacco and loincloths. Islamic invaders were birds of passage. Most of the European empires were short-lived, but it was the Europeans who transformed the continent.

[4] *African World*, May 1967.

CHAPTER III

Muslim Colonialism

It is customary and convenient to divide Africa, like Caesar's Gaul, into three parts. The great desert, stretching from the Red Sea across the continent to Senegal, separates Mediterranean Africa, the Africa of Jewry, Christendom and Islam, from the Africa of the Negro. South of the Zambesi lies the third Africa, where Europeans have put down roots and have built and maintained a civilisation not merely for quick profit but for posterity.

From the Red Sea, from the Nile, and perhaps from pre-Muslim Yemen, sprang the early "Sudanic"[1] dynasties. These imposed themselves on still earlier agricultural societies, and brought them new ways of commerce, mining and metallurgy. Christianity spread from Meroitic Egypt to Nubia and beyond. The Sahara was often a refuge from persecution of the Faith.

In the fourth century, two Roman boys, Edesius and Frumentius, were captured at the Red Sea port of Axum—present-day Ethiopia—which, with its great ivory market and capital, castles and royal tombs, with the largest monolith in the world, was a considerable emporium and centre of civilised life. The captive boys grew up in Axum and then were allowed to return to Rome. Frumentius was ordained priest, returned and converted King Azana of Axum to Christianity. The Christian Ethiopian Emperors claimed descent from Solomon the Wise through

[1] Sudan means "country of the blacks".

20

Menelik, his son by the Queen of Sheba. Axum was "Zion" and the "second Jerusalem". About A.D. 300 its territories stretched from the White Nile to the Somali coast and the Persian Gulf.

From the second century of our era Arabs were ranging across the East African littoral. They brought the Faith of Mohammed into the Sudan from the Yemen, Arabia's heartland, and Arabs settled in the territories, now known as Somalia, Kenya and Tanzania. Kilwa, Mombasa, Lamu and Mogadishu were to become their chief trading centres.

Armed with Koran and sword, their wanderlust fed by the works of Ptolemy translated into Arabic, the apostles of Islam constructed a vast, brilliant and cosmopolitan system which stretched from the Iberian Peninsular to the Indus Valley, and from the Caspian Sea to south of the Sahara. The Arab conquest of North Africa was long and arduous. The Roman conquerors of Phoenician Carthage had brought the southern shores of *Mare Nostrum* within an empire which later acknowledged the *imperium* of Christ. St. Augustine, the great Father of the Roman Church, was a Berber of Numidia, in what is now modern Tunisia. His people resisted the invading Arabs with the desperate courage that their later conquerors, the French, experienced in their turn. The Berbers were converted to Islam only to lapse and be re-converted, for, according to Ibn Khaldun, they apostasised twelve times. But finally, Okba bin Nafi, the founder in A.D. 670 of the holy city of Kairouan, whose mosques the Tunisians are restoring for tourists, reached the Atlantic and, we are told, spurred his horse into the waves, summoning Allah to witness that he had redeemed his oath to take Islam to the end of the civilised world, which was Morocco.

The desert men brought the desert with them. When the

21

Fatimite Caliph of Cairo diverted the Hilalian Arabs to the *Maghreb*,[2] Arabs and converted Berbers wrecked Roman aqueducts, dams and cisterns. Ibn Khaldun commented acidly in the *Muqaddima* :

> "Since the irruption of the Banu Hilal and Banu Sulaym into Ifriqiya and the *Maghreb* at the beginning of the fifth century . . . these plains, where civilisation blossomed from the Sudan to the Caspian Sea, have been utterly devastated. The rubble of monuments and buildings, the traces of villages and farms bear witness."

After the subjection of North Africa, Berber and Arab turned to the subjection of Spain. At the same time their horsemen swung south, and carried Islam to Sijilmasa, which controlled the gold route from West Africa, and thence to the banks of the Niger and Senegal rivers. The gold-rich empire of Ghana was overrun.

From the destruction of Ghana sprang the rule of the kings of Mali, known in Egypt as Tekrur, whose sway extended from Senegal to the oases south of Algeria and the loop of the Niger. Their prosperity largely derived from the trans-Saharan traffic in gold and salt.

Timbuktu, named after a slave girl, was the capital of Mali. Here ruled the great emperor Mansa Musa. As architect for his city he appointed the Andalusian poet Es-Saheli, who built of burnt bricks a mosque which survived three centuries later. To this city flocked literati and divines, jurists and merchants. The Mansa (sultan) died in 1332. Under his successor, his nephew Maghan, the empire continued to flourish, to judge from the report of Ibn Battuta in 1335 :

> "There is complete security in the country. Neither traveller nor inhabitant . . . has anything to fear from robbers or men of violence."

[2] *Maghreb* is Arabic for west. North Africa was the Arab west.

Kingship was firm and just and Leo Africanus—Hassan ben Muhammad el Wazzan es Zayyati—thought that the Mali negroes excelled all others in wit, civility and industry.

When Mansa Musa embarked on his famous pilgrimage to Mecca, he gave a fillip to trade between the Sudan, the *Maghreb* and Egypt. Under his rule, Timbuktu grew into a great commercial centre, and the chief *entrepôt* for *tibar* (gold dust). The Catalan atlas of Charles V, drawn by Abraham Cresque of Majorca *circa* 1379 is inscribed:

> "This negro lord is called Musa Mali, Lord of the Negroes of Guinea. So abundant is the gold which is found in his country that he is the richest and most noble king in all the land."

Similar wording adorned the Majorcan planisphere of Mercia de Viladestro (1413).

Empires do not last. Around the middle Niger, Muhammad Turré, the founder of the Abkia dynasty which ruled from Gao, on the River Niger, stirred up the warlike Songhai, who had been vassals of Mali, into aggression against her. Seventy leopard-skin bags held Muhammad Turré's robes, and when in 1495–1497 he went on *haj* (pilgrimage), his alms were 300,000 pieces of gold. Under him worked four viceroys and his state was served by a systematic administration for police, taxation and weights and measures. The Songhai had a standing army and a rudimentary navy. Their king canalised the middle course of the Niger, gave land to Jewish refugees fleeing from persecution in Tuat, and traded with merchants from Tripolitania. The Caliph of Egypt conferred on him the title of "Representative of the Prince of the Faithful".

In 1505, the Songhai invaded Mali and in 1546 the imperial palace at Timbuktu was sacked. Under their hegemony, however, both Timbuktu and Jenne flowered both intellectually and spiritually. Leo Africanus was impressed by the lecturers who were attracted from Cairo as well as Fez to teach Muslim theology and law, rhetoric, grammar and literature. But invasion by the Moroccans in 1590 struck a deadly blow from which the Western Sudan never recovered, and a period of anarchy opened as bloody as that of the reign of King Stephen in England. The Songhai could not withstand the artillery of the Moroccans.

The Songhai constituted the second Muslim system of the Sudan. The third was that of the Hausa states, pre-eminently that which had Kano as its capital and received the Islamic faith when the potentate Yeji (1349–1385) was converted from Mali.

Caravans carried the Faith, as well as the gold of the Upper Niger, the copper of Agadir and the slaves of Guiné. Usually, however, it was men of substance and importance who were converted. Lesser folk would cling, like the pagans of Christendom, to a belief in the old spirits and local divinities. Islam only adorned the surface of Negro life and manners.

The Sudanic economy was mainly rural and pastoral. More urbanised societies were found among the Akan, and other peoples of Guiné. Mande merchants throve. Benin, on the Gold Coast, well-known for its art, was famed in Europe. The Dutch geographer, Olfert Dapper, reported in his *Description of Africa* in 1668, of the visit of a group of Dutch merchants from the Low Countries.

> "The King's palace," they reported, "is on the right side of the town . . . a collection of buildings which occupy as much space as the town of Harlem."[3]

Nor were the Bantu all or always backward. Ibn Battuta described the beauty of the city of Kilwa in Tanzania. In

[3] Davidson, Basil: *op. cit.*

24

Somalia, this great explorer found a state comparable to those he had encountered in the southern Sahara. Medieval geographers knew of the land of Zinj, whose name survives in Zanzibar. This coastal state, facing the Indian Ocean, received Arab, Persian and Indian merchants during the Middle Ages. The early sixteenth century Kings of Kilwa claimed to be descended from Persian monarchs. The historian Basil Davidson describes it as "a true Venice of the South".

Portugal's first contacts with African kingdoms are equally revealing. When the Portuguese discovered the Congo they found an intelligent people, eager to trade and receptive of the Gospel. In Mashonaland, Mocasanga, which they sometimes described as Monomotapa, from the imperial title of the priest monarchy, was an organised state when they arrived, trading in gold through Sofala in Mozambique. The ruins of Zimbabwe recall a culture that reached its peak between the ninth and the thirteenth centuries, and display what Philip Mason[4] calls "a sudden spurt of progress".

There were many reasons why, south of the Sahara, Africa could not develop this early promise. The horsemen and cameleers of the Sudanic empires and states—Ghana, Mali, Gao, Hausaland, Bornu, Kanem, Darfur, Sennar, Ethiopia and Adel—crossed and re-crossed the deserts to the Mediterranean lands. East Africa was connected to the north by dhow. Inland however, and southward from the Sudan, the tsetse fly halted the nomadic horsemen at the forest belt, and the mosquito drained their health and vitality.

"The movement was on foot or by canoe, all land transport on the human head and shoulder. Not until the very late

[4] Mason, Philip: *The Birth of a Dilemma: The Conquest and Settlement of Rhodesia*, O.U.P. 1958.

25

nineteenth century were even European resources sufficient
to overcome these isolating factors."[5]

Successive states were broken and plundered by migrant
brigand invaders; their buildings were eaten by termites.
Roland Oliver likens to the Vandals and Visigoths

"the Zimbas who swept up the east coast of Africa in the
late sixteenth century, the Jugas who harried the Congo
kingdoms in the seventeenth century, and the various Zulu
hordes which in the early nineteenth century streamed
northwards from Natal, incorporating new members from
every tribe they passed *en route*, and settling finally as the
Matabele of Southern Rhodesia, the Shangaans of Southern
Mozambique and Tanzania. . . . It was perhaps the greatest
weakness of African monarchies that they never hit upon
the principle of primogeniture, nor upon any other certain
system of succession. It was in deciding upon a succession
to the chieftainship that stability was most severely
threatened, and that more powerful states found their best
opportunities of intervening in the affairs of their weaker
neighbours."[6]

It was in this "moment of great confusion" that the first
Europeans arrived.

[5] Oliver, Roland: *op. cit.*
[6] Oliver, Roland: *op. cit.*

CHAPTER IV

Portugal Leads

Portuguese involvement in Africa goes back to that period of the late Middle Ages when the Arabs were finally driven from the Iberian peninsula and were pursued across the Straits of Gibraltar by Portuguese forces determined to protect their homeland by the best defence of all—attack. The port of Tangier became a scene of triumphant siege and disastrous defeat.

In Chaucer's lifetime, John of Gaunt had renewed the ancient English alliance with the Christian powers of Portugal and Castile. Knights from England had taken part in the liberation of Lisbon from its Moorish overlords and a priest from Sussex, Gilbert of Hastings, was consecrated as the city's bishop. In 1415, the year of Agincourt, a band of English knights accompanied John of Gaunt's grandson, the *Infante* Henrique, better known as Prince Henry the Navigator, on an expedition to the North African town of Ceuta and there helped to win for Portugal her first foothold in Africa. Thus the Anglo-Portuguese alliance, cemented by the marriage of John I to Philippa of Lancaster, which created the line of Avis, helped the scion of the two seafaring kingdoms to lay the foundations of the first oceanic empire of Europe.

The half-English navigator was part medieval crusader; part child of the Renaissance. Withdrawing from the life of the Portuguese court, this bold, blond ascetic, a man of faith, vision and scientific system gathered to his service at

27

Vila do Infante, his retreat near Cape St. Vincent, captains, cartographers and pilots.

Christopher Columbus studied there at the Castle of Sagres, later to be sacked by Sir Francis Drake, and before embarking on his own voyages for the rival court of Ferdinand and Isabella, Columbus served Portugal in the mines of the Gold Coast. Here was built the caravel—a vessel which, with its lateen sail, owed much to the Arabs, as did the astrolabe, the principal instrument in navigation. Shipyards for the construction of these boats were set up at Lisbon, Lagos, and Faro.

The *Infante de Sagres*, as Prince Henry was known, sought a route to the riches of the East outflanking the Saracens, for it was the Moors rather than the Venetians who held the gorgeous East in fee. Their middlemen decreed the price the West had to pay for spices. Medieval princes had hoped to ally with the Mongols and force the Muslims to fight on two fronts. Hope was now placed in the St. Thomas Christians of Malabar and on Prester John, the legendary ruler of a Christian kingdom hidden in the wilds of Africa. Envoys of Prester John appeared in Portugal in 1427 and 1450, and contact between the Holy See and Ethiopia had been established early in the fourteenth century.

Moorish prisoners told the Navigator of the caravan routes to Tunis, Timbuktu, the Senegal, thought of at the time as the Western Nile, Cantor, the rich rice emporium on the Gambia, and to the Gold Coast. Doubtless, these Arab caravans brought tales of an African Rio Doro or River of Gold—an *El Dorado* said to flow through Bilad Ghana (or Guiné). The region had already appeared on the *Catalan Map* of 1375 and it was known to Jewish traders; but since Portugal, unlike most European kingdoms, had no gold

28

currency of her own, there was added to the crusading impulse the urge to divert gold dust from the camel caravans of the western Sudan and from the Muslim middlemen of Barbary to fill her own coffers. Surrounded by Muslim Africa, Portugal realised that she must outflank the great western promentory to reach Guiné, outflank Guiné to reach Southern Africa, and round the Cape to outflank Africa itself in order to reach the "Spice Islands" of the Indies.

The conversion of unbelievers, including the pagan Negroes of Senegambia, anywhere between Morocco and the Indies, was authorised by the Holy See[1]. The papal bull *Inter Cetera*, published in 1456, stated that for the previous twenty-five years Portuguese caravels had sailed southwards to the West Coast of Africa, arrived at the Gambia, and discovered the mouth of the Senegal—wrongly described as the Nile.

Portuguese progress down the African coast was slow and cautious. It was nearly two decades after Agincourt and Ceuta that a squire of Prince Henry, Gil Eannes, returned to his prince bearing St. Mary's roses picked south of Cape Bojador, the margin of the Green Sea of Dragons, and other terrors. Before a Tudor was enthroned in England, the King of Portugal was styled, by papal permission, Lord of Guiné. This title was to last as long as the monarchy. The Pope gave Prince Henry the monopoly of enterprise beyond Cape Bojador, and the Prince's explorers touched successively Sierra Leone and the Gold Coast (the modern, not the ancient, Ghana) and erected their characteristic stone pillars at the mouth of the Congo estuary.

Portugal's presence in Guiné dates from 1448. She dis-

[1] In 1494 Pope Alexander VI approved the Treaty of Tordisillas. This divided the world outside Europe between Portugal and Spain.

covered the then uninhabited Cape Verde Islands in 1460. The Portuguese coastal castles of São Jorge da Mina (Elmina) and Axem were built in 1481 and 1503, respectively, for defence against Spanish and other European interlopers and to impress and overawe the tribes from whom the Portuguese obtained their gold. Portugal occupied the islands of São Tome and Principe from 1470. Her explorers were in Angola in 1482.

In 1488 the Cape of Good Hope was what its name declared, for, on rounding it, Bartholomeu Dias reported the sea route to the Indies opened. Dias' ambition encompassed the gold of Solomon's Ophir, the Indies trade, and the salvation of souls. Like Vasco da Gama, he sought "Christians and spices".

In the same year an Arabic-speaking squire, Pero de Covilhan, reached the west coast of India, continuing to the Persian Gulf and the Swahili coast of East Africa. This momentous journey took him two years to accomplish. He was in Cairo on his way home when he received word from the "perfect prince", Dom Joâo II, who had succeeded Dom Afonso V on the Portuguese throne, and shared with his great ancestor a passion for Africa. The King's message ordered de Covilhan to go in search of Prester John.

This legendary Christian emperor had been originally located in the Indies—this term embracing Ethiopia and East Africa as well as India proper. King John had hoped to find him via the Senegal, the Gambia and then the Zaire (Congo). Each of these great rivers was in its turn mistaken for a tributary or a branch of the Nile. Yet every southward advance made by the Portuguese brought, not penetration of the continent, but circumnavigation. For :

"in all the entrances of the great Ethiopia that we navigate along, he has placed a striking angel with a flaming sword

30

of deadly fever which prevents us from penetrating into the interior to the empires of the garden, where prevail these rivers of gold that flow to the sea in so many parts of the continent."[2]

However, Pero de Covilhan eventually arrived at the court of Prester John in the Abyssinian highlands in 1493. The Negus received him with honour, gave him a wife but never allowed him to return to Portugal. He died in Ethiopia two years later.

Following in the path of Vasco da Gama, the viceroys d'Almeida and de Albuquerque established Portuguese predominance north-east from the Cape. De Albuquerque became Governor of India in 1503, and it was during his term of office that the greatest Portuguese conquests were made. On the coast of the Indian Ocean, the Portuguese outgunned and outfought their Arab rivals, who had been in business at Kilwa and elsewhere since the eighth century A.D., and wrested from them the trade in gold, ivory and gum. Mozambique Island was occupied in 1507 and became the first European settlement in sub-Saharan Africa, including amongst its inhabitants Indians and Ismailis, as well as Africans and Europeans. Until recently the island was the capital of the Portuguese province of Mozambique. Its Fortress of St. Sebastian enshrines the oldest Christian church in East Africa beyond the Sahara. St. Francis Xavier celebrated mass in a smaller church. Through the island passed da Gama, Magellan and Portugal's epic poet, Camões—for this was the way to the Indies and to Japan.

In 1509 d'Almeida sank the Turkish fleet in a battle at Diu, north of Bombay, and opened the Red Sea port of Massawa to the Portuguese. In 1520, they sent a diplomatic mission to Ethiopia. This was followed by Turkish attack

[2] Boxer, C. R.: *Four Centuries of Portuguese Expansion 1415–1825.*

31

and conquest, forcing a Christian remnant into the mountains. In 1541 a son of da Gama, Dom Christopher, broke through the Turkish blockade, only to die on his way up-country. However, a survivor from his forces made gunpowder from local sulphur and saltpetre and, thus armed, the Ethiopians wiped out the Turks near Lake Tsana.[3]

In general, the absence of inland waterways and the lethal ubiquity of the malaria-carrying mosquito hemmed the Portuguese in on the shores of the ocean. Penetration of the interior continued to be spasmodic. The first European to venture far into the hinterland of Southern Africa appears to have been a *degredado* (banished criminal). António Fernandes was sent from Lisbon to report on the sources of the gold reaching the sea at Sofala. He accordingly set out in 1541 towards Zimbabwe, undeterred by Arab and allied African attacks on Sofala itself. The gold workings and gold trading of the empire of the "great plunderer", Mwene Mtapa (Monomotapa),[4] raised hopes of finding Ophir and King Solomon's mines. António Fernandes reached the Sabi valley.

Other Portuguese explorers to reach what is now Rhodesia were impressed by the barbaric culture of Monomotapa's empire. Persian carpets and Chinese porcelain were displayed. They saw hundreds of stone *zimbabwes*—chieftains' tombs. Duarte Barbosa wrote of the empire's formidable army, with its corps of Amazons.

In 1561, Rhodesia gained its first Christian martyr, when Gonçalo da Silveira, a Jesuit, was murdered in Mashonaland, where his zeal had aroused Muslim hostility and the suspicions of a Monomotapa. In 1569, King Sebastian of Portugal sent Francisco Barreto to conquer the interior.

---

[3] "Ethiopia was saved by 450 Portuguese" [Gibbon].
[4] Master of the ravaged lands.

He failed, but later expeditions established Portugal in Manicaland. Amongst Rhodesian legends is the punitive expedition of 300 Portuguese arquebusiers in 1632, when a cross shone resplendent in the sky, though lacking a divine wording such as that which sealed the victory of Constantine at the Milvian bridge. Monomotapa became a client of Portugal and, despite disease and distance, the attempt to colonise Rhodesia only faded into obscurity as Brazil and India claimed Portuguese soldiers and resources.

On the other side of the continent, Portugal, for a time, took deeper root. The Congo was discovered by Diogo Cão, and a converted Christian king, Dom Afonso I (1506–43), adopted the Faith, manners and court ceremonial of his protectors. In the year that Columbus sailed westwards in his attempt to reach the Indies, two Germans set up a printing press in the Congo. Portuguese women came there to teach homecraft. Two Congolese princes went on embassy to the Vatican. One of them, Dom Henrique, was consecrated titular Bishop of Utica, in Tunisia, at the instance of King Manoel of Portugal. In 1521, Bishop Henrique returned to the Congo accompanied by a missionary band of Negro ordinands. Artisans were sent from Portugal, together with a farmer to break in oxen, and to teach the art of cheese making—"because all the milk there goes to waste".

The kingdom of Manicongo set a pattern for Luso-Portuguese assimilation. Unfortunately, in Angola, the Portuguese fell out with the Congolese. When the Dutch occupied Luanda (1641–48), the Congolese sided with the invaders, though they rejected their Calvinism. Thus, the battle of Ambuila in 1665 was fought between two Catholic armies. The King of the Congo fell in action. Anarchy resulted, and, ever since, São Salvador, the capital of the "Portuguese

c

33

Congo", has been dwarfed by bustling São Paulo de Luanda.

Portuguese colonial philosophy during this period was however largely mercantilist. Portugal had neither the man-power nor the resources to exploit continents. She concen-trated on holding the sea-ports, and establishing good re-lations with the native rulers. Hers was a policy of trade and not of conquest. Though her commerce was sometimes discreditable—the trade in "black ivory" (slaves) was second in importance only to that in gold—Portugal set a pattern for civilised relationships with native African rulers that other European powers would have done well to copy.

Prince Henry the Navigator and the clash of crusade with *jihad*[5] had set forces moving which were still felt in Africa four centuries later. The waves of Portuguese and Arab enterprise were stirring the waters of the great lakes at the same time as Shaka Zulu's devil wind—*Mfecane*—was blowing scorchingly from the south to devour two million people, and the friction of the British was displac-ing the Boer to keep his historic rendezvous with the Bantu.[6]

[5] Religious war.

[6] "Be-ntu" means a people linked by language and custom. Those thus called were given the name by Dr. W. H. I. Bleck at the sug-gestion of Sir George Grey, Governor of the Cape Colony, in the 1850's.

CHAPTER V

The Scramble

Meanwhile, far to the south, the Boers were also on the move. In 1752, a vanguard of *trekkers* encountered Ngoni tribesmen for the first time.

The name "Boer", which means "farmer", goes back to the first Dutch settlers of the Cape of Good Hope. In 1652, Jan van Riebeeck made Cape Town a port of call for the ships of the Netherlands East India Company, and built a fort to defend it. Germans and exiled Huguenots from France reinforced the Dutch. As early as 1691 the second generation of South African-born whites outnumbered those born in Europe.

The Cape fell to the British as a prize of the Revolutionary and the Napoleonic Wars. One of the fruits of victory at Waterloo was heavy unemployment and, to relieve this, the first organised scheme of British emigration planted the 1820 British Settlers.

The Boers, for their part, resented British tutelage and officialdom, personified by the overbearing personality of Lord Charles Somerset, the emancipation of the Hottentots by the Acts of 1828 and 1833, and the ending of slavery with insufficient compensation. Mutual distrust led to many Boers moving into the interior. The view of the emigrants was thus stated : "We despair of saving the colony from those evils that threaten it, by the turbulent and dishonest conduct of vagabonds who are allowed to infest the country in every part." In any case, it was said that a true Boer

35

felt crowded if he could see the smoke from his neighbour's chimney. In 1799, the *trekkers* met Bantu of the Xhosa nation at the Great Fish River. A long period of "Kaffir" wars was to follow. The Great Trek of 1836–7 was the exordium to an epic which Harold Macmillan described, in his speech to the Union Parliament in 1960, as "the first of the African nationalisms". The then Prime Minister continued :

> "You are sprung from Europe, the home of nationalism, and here in Africa you have yourselves created a new nationalism."

The Great Trek was an act of repudiation of the world outside Africa. The Boers were a peculiar people, their staple reading the Bible in High Dutch. Like the Children of Israel, they passed through the Wilderness, Amalakite-beset, but there was no Moses. Families fended for themselves to reach their Promised Land. More than 10,000 folk, nearly a quarter of the European population of Cape Colony, with their servants, joined the exodus. Ancestral homes were abandoned; farms were sold for a song. The Boers trekked across the Orange River out of Cape Colony. They marched on through the future Orange Free State into the Northern Transvaal. Britain's command of the sea saved Natal for the Crown, the colony being annexed in May 1843. The *trekkers* were joined by both foreign and English-speaking pioneers and Scots and Dutch Calvinist pastors. Hunters, traders and prospectors from the Transvaal entered what was later to be known as Southern Rhodesia and there entered into competition with the Portuguese from Angola, who had voyaged into the interior via the Zambesi.

Most of Africa, however, remained an enigma. The crusading and colonising fervour of the Catholic powers was spent by the end of the sixteenth century. It was discouraging for the Portuguese when, after they had given aid to Ethiopia in her struggle against the Muslims, the country was closed to Europeans by an edict of the Negus. The Coptic Church resented Jesuit missionary enthusiasm.

Indeed dreams of an *El Dorado* found more material fulfilment in South America than in Africa. Zimbabwe was nothing more than an impressive ruin. Coasts beset by mangrove swamp or by barren desert were uninviting. The mosquito was merciless. Only the slave trade boomed, but the chiefs who profited from it wanted no interlopers and discouraged all attempts to venture into the interior. Most of the European journeys of the seventeenth and the early eighteenth centuries were confined to the slaving rivers of the Senegal, the Gambia or the Calabar. The sources of the Niger and the Nile remained unsolved mysteries.

Britain's loss of her American Colonies, after the first great U.D.I. of 1776, aroused new interest in Africa. There were rumours of a hitherto undiscovered civilisation on the Niger. The fabled wealth of Timbuktu was a potent mirage.

Before the days of the Suez Canal, morever, Africa lay directly across the route to Asia, where "John Company" was carving out a new empire for Britain to replace that lost in the Americas. The private enterprise of a Mungo Park or a Mary Kingsley attracted State support. The younger Pitt placed the resources of the Consular Service at the disposal of the African Association.

This scientific and commercial body was formed in 1788 under the presidency of Sir Joseph Banks, a botanist who had accompanied Cook on his Pacific voyages. Banks now transferred his curiosity from the Pacific Ocean to the Dark Continent. Wilberforce was a member of the Association, as were Wedgwood, Fox and Clarkson—for the Clapham Sect saw the opportunity to use the Association in their campaign to force the abolition of slavery.

Slavery having been declared illegal in Britain herself in 1786, a number of Negroes, who had exchanged slavery for poverty, were resettled at Freetown in Sierra Leone. In 1791, they were reinforced by a band of American Negroes, who had remained loyal to King George and after Yorktown had settled and freezed in Nova Scotia. A ship-load of whores was sent to keep them company. The Committee for the Relief of Poor Blacks, which had sponsored the colonisation, became the Sierra Leone Company, which marched in step with the African Association.

It is said that the Gold Coast originated with the slave trade. In 1807, however, Great Britain outlawed it completely, and for the rest of the century her men-of-war patrolled the West Coast of Africa. Forced to turn to trading in other commodities, traders saw little reason to continue to deal through the native chiefs, who had acted as middle-men, and began to press inland.

The Royal Africa Company controlled English affairs in Gambia, where the ghostly ruin of Fort James up-river commemorates the enterprise of James, Duke of York, and the versatile as well as dashing Prince Rupert in the seventeenth century. Gambia became a Crown Colony in 1843. The colony of Lagos was ceded to Britain in 1861, but it was not until the Berlin Conference of 1885 that a British protectorate over the interior was recognised by the other great powers.

The motives of British Imperialism were commercial, humanitarian and scientific. Mary Kingsley knew that trade would bring Africa face to face with Western civilisation, and enable her tribes to break the bounds of fear and fetish. The heroic career of David Livingstone was inspired by the

38

twin causes of "Commerce and Christianity". Stanley spoke more coarsely of "philanthropy at five per cent". Trade in goods was to replace trade in fellow human beings.

African tribal authority, however, could seldom ensure the enforcement of the law and order necessary for such a traffic to flourish. The chartered companies began to add administrative functions to their original commercial purposes. For the Home Government was usually reluctant to become too deeply involved in the affairs of the Dark Continent. Africa was a relatively minor field of investment. Demands for intervention, political protection, or outright annexation, came not so much from politicians or the merchants of the City of London, as from explorers, missionaries and African potentates themselves.

Britain's hand was forced by the need to secure the route to India, "that brightest jewel in the Imperial Crown", against the ambitions of other expansionist empires. The Germain *Reich* was resurgent. France, humiliated in Europe by Germany with the annexation of Alsace-Lorraine in 1871, looked to Africa for the balm of gain and glory. United Italy too coveted "a place in the sun".

As for the Germans, they stole a march on the British in the Cameroons. In 1879, five chiefs petitioned Queen Victoria, in what they called "a nice long letter", to be annexed by the British :

> "Plenty wars here in our country, plenty murder, and plenty idol-worshippers."

Their pleas to the British Consul had been repeatedly ignored.

> "When we knew about Calabar River, how they all have English laws in their towns, and how they have put away all their superstitions, oh, we shall be very glad to be like Calabar River."

39

In 1876, the Bechuanas too asked for the Queen's protection against the Boers, but decisive action was not taken until after the Boer War.

France had held Senegal since 1637, apart from short periods of seizure by English or Dutch fleets. Goree was added in 1697, and the energetic General Faidherbe, posted in disgrace to Senegal under the Second Empire in 1854, conquered the interior eastward and southward as far as the British posts on the Gambia, and later founded the magnificent port of Dakar. In 1830, Algeria was annexed by Louis-Philippe, and the Third Republic secured "compensation" for Gladstone's "temporary" occupation of Egypt by asserting her protectorate over the Bey of Tunis and by pursuing a vigorous "forward" colonial policy on the Niger. Italy occupied Asab and became mistress of Eritrea but Ethiopa contrived to keep her imperial independence.

Nor would the Belgians be left out. Henry Morton Stanley said :

"since history teaches that colonies are useful, that they play a great part in that which makes up the power and prosperity of states, let us strive to get one in our turn . . . let us see where there are unoccupied lands, where are to be found peoples to civilise, to lead to progress in every sense, meanwhile ensuring ourselves new revenues, to our middle classes the employment which they seek, to our army a little activity, and to Belgium as a whole the opportunity to prove to the world that it is also an imperial people capable of dominating and enlightening others."

King Leopold II summoned the Brussels Conference of 1876, which led to the establishment of the largely Belgian International Africa Association, the dispatch of H. M. Stanley to the Congo, and the establishment of the Congo Free State. The invention of the pneumatic tyre meant that there was profit in rubber.

40

A later international conference in Berlin, in 1884, adopted a resolution on the slave trade, declared its belief in the virtues of Free Trade, an ethic which most of the colonial powers swiftly proceeded to deny by their actions, and declared the need to prove effective occupation of a territory before declaring it annexed. This did not deter Bismarck from announcing, while the conference was sitting, a German protectorate over parts of East Africa, where Karl Peters had made a series of treaties with the native chiefs. South-West Africa, Kamarun and Togoland became German.

The "scramble for Africa" was on. To check German expansion, Lord Salisbury in 1886 marked out the spheres of British influence in East Africa. By agreement with Germany, Zanzibar came under British control in 1891. At the same time Britain relinquished her claims in Madagascar in favour of those of France.

The anti-slavery theme in European colonialism recurred at the Brussels Conference of 1889. The powers agreed to prosecute the crusade against slavery, which had been preached throughout Europe by Cardinal Lavigerie, founder of the first house of White Fathers, more properly known as the *Société des Missionaires de Notre Dame d'Afrique*, in Algiers in 1871. Livingstone's old associate, Sir John Kirk, secured from the sixteen signatories of the Berlin Act, which emerged from the conference in 1885, an agreement to suppress the trade in slaves, arms and liquor throughout Southern Africa. The Berlin Act served to justify British and French expeditions against Arab slave empires in the Sudan, and round the Niger and Lake Chad.

Meanwhile, the vision of the sickly son of a Hertfordshire clergyman ranged from the Cape to Cairo. In 1887,

41

Cecil Rhodes won control of the De Beers mine at Kimberley. His company, The Consolidated Gold Fields of South Africa Ltd., became a means to achieve Rhodes' imperial dreams. Rhodes could not reign supreme in Johannesburg, but he hoped for a second Rand beyond the Limpopo, where his writ would run unquestioned. The Biblical Ophir was thought to lie there, and Rider Haggard set his novel *King Solomon's Mines* in Rhodesia.

But Germans in the West and the East, and the Portuguese, desirous of linking Angola with Mozambique in effective occupation, threatened to close a road that Rhodes believed that Briton and Boer alike should tread together. If President Kruger's Transvaal joined hands with the Germans, the way northwards would be barred.

"The Suez Canal into the interior" was Bechuanaland. Joseph Chamberlain at the Colonial Office sent Sir Charles Warren to secure it. In 1887, the British High Commissioner at the Cape entered into treaty relations with Lobengula, Chief of the Matabele, who had fled before Shaka's Zulu *impis* and scourged the milder Mashona with their raids. In the following year, Rhodes obtained, through the Rudd Concession, the monopoly of all mineral rights in Lobengula's kingdom. In 1889, the British South Africa Company received its Royal Charter to promote trade, commerce, civilization and good government in the area lying immediately north of British Bechuanaland.

In 1890, a pioneer column from South Africa, escorted by B.S.A. police, hoisted the Union Jack at Harare, in what is now Cecil Square, Salisbury. Rival Transvaaler *trekkers* were checked, and in 1891, the Charter was extended to the Congo, although Katanga fell under Belgian jurisdiction. The foundation of the Rhodesias had been laid.

Rhodes's reputation was tarnished by the Jameson Raid

—or was it by its humiliating failure? Nor are the talents of the imperialist financier those most eulogised nowadays in press and pulpit. "Philanthropy at five per cent" is an even more unfashionable notion than Livingstone's "Commerce and Christianity". Yet when Rhodes's restless, complex spirit passed away in 1902 the Archbishop of Cape Town committed no excess of panegyric in quoting King David's question after the death of Abner : "Know ye not that there is a prince and a great man fallen this day in Israel?"[1] So much so that a brief assessment of Rhodes's achievement in Southern Africa should be attempted.

By cash and conspiracy, annexations and scholarships Rhodes strove with all his energies, his riches and the short space given him ("So much to do, so little done") to unify Southern Africa under the Union Jack and within a British Empire that might in alliance with the United States of America and even Imperial Germany—there were German as well as Empire and American Rhodes Scholars—keep the peace of the world. Other national flags than the British now fly, even in Rhodesia (save on Pioneer Day in Cecil Square, Salisbury); and instead of an all-red Cape to Cairo route through what was then German Tanganyika there are the makings of a line of subversion from Cairo to Cape—all-red in another sense. Nevertheless the unity of the "Dutch" with the English-speaking South Africans for which he worked with his friend Jan Hofmeyr has largely come about and so has the modern industrial power of Rhodes's vision.

It was to remove obstacles to that vision that he annexed Pondoland and destroyed the kingdom of Lobengula. Yet the courage and patience with which he pacified the Matabele in revolt earned Rhodes unprecedented royal honours at his death. His Glen Grey Act forshadowed the territorial

[1] II Samuel, iii, 38 (A.V.).

separation of the tribal Africans. For the detribalised and literate, indeed "for all civilised men" there should be "equal rights", and the Native Reserves themselves should be a means of education as well as of protection for the primitive. "Education," he held, "is the whole difference between barbarism and civilisation." If his world-view was sometimes crude and contradictory, it was in essence noble and never mean.

In East Africa, missionaries of rival persuasions and companies of competing nationalities played their part in spreading the bounds of empire still wider. The 1890 agreement with Germany endorsed Britain's position in Uganda, Kenya, Zanzibar and on the western shores of Lake Nyasa. In 1895, Britain undertook to build a railway from Mombasa to Lake Victoria to facilitate the final suppression of the slave trade. It accomplished this purpose, and also served to open up the Kenya Highlands, which were sparsely populated though salubrious.

French penetration of West Africa from the Senegal river brought about a similar delineation of West African frontiers. The boundaries of the British Gambia Protectorate were marked out in 1889, and those of Sierre Leone in 1895. British control now spread from the westernised Negroes and Creoles of the Coast to the inland tribes. In Ashanti, Prempeh was deposed. The only proof of civilisation that Joseph Chamberlain could find in him was "that he has engaged a London solicitor to advance his interests". Not that the Little Englanders, as those who opposed imperial advance were contemptuously labelled, were deterred from protesting at Imperialist aggression against this "barbarous chief who has permitted human sacrifices, attacked friendly chiefs and broken a treaty". Another war was waged by Britain against Benin in the Oil Rivers Protectorate, on the

West Coast of Africa. The naval landing party found the King's palace reeking with the blood of sacrifices.

In 1893, Colonel (afterwards Marshal) Joffre relieved at Timbuktu a French force beleaguered by Tuareg Arabs. Senegal was linked by rail to the Niger. The French also subdued Dahomey and its eight hundred Amazons. From there, they moved south down the Niger, into the kingdom of Borgu, there to be forestalled by the rapid marching of Lugard, brought from East Africa by George Taubman Goldie. The Emirates of Nupe and Ilorin fell to Britain.

Goldie was an extraordinary man. He had resigned his military commission "without troubling to send in his papers", and according to his own account, lived three years with the Bedouin for his love of an Arab maid. Enjoying private means, he never took a penny from the Royal Niger Company, or any other enterprise he directed. He attacked the liquor trade as well as slavers. In 1890, negotiations with the French over the region of the Niger gave Goldie the rich Emirates of Nupe and Ilorin, leaving the French with what Salisbury sardonically described as "a very light soil". Goldie, the maker of Nigeria, abolished slavery through a tract of land three times the size of Great Britain.

An Englishman and a Frenchman completed Europe's long struggle of atonement against the Arab slave trade in Central Africa. The Frenchman, Colonel Lamy—the enemy of the notorious slaver, Rabeh—was killed in a victory won south of Lake Chad in 1902. Fort Lamy perpetuates his name. The Englishman was Sir Frederick (later Lord) Lugard, a knight of Empire imbued with a sense of duty to mankind. He had fought a private war against the Arab slavers near Lake Nyasa. As a soldier and administrator, he had served in Afghanistan, Egypt, Burma, on both sides of Africa and in Hong Kong. After making a journey through the Kalahari desert for Rhodes, he was recalled by Goldie to take command of the West African Frontier Force. In 1900, the Crown took over in Northern Nigeria, and Lugard, as Commissioner, was sent to pacify the Hausa and the Fulani Emirs. He took by storm the walled cities of Kano and Sokoto.

The ambitions of France to join the Atlantic and Indian Oceans to the Mediterranean under the tricolor had the brevity of a night's dream. In 1898, the Anglo-French frontier from Lake Chad to Senegal was marked out on the map. There were, however, some variations from the previously accepted line of 1840. No sooner had the 1898 agreement been signed than Major J. B. Marchand, a French officer, was reported to be at Fashoda. His complicated four-year journey had been inspired by Gabriel Hanotaux, a statesman with no love for Britain who thought, in the largest possible terms, of breaking her Cape to Cairo axis with a wedge driven from Senegal to Somaliland. Unfortunately for France, the British had already advanced up the Nile to avenge General Gordon and chastise his Mahdist murderers, and soon after Kitchener's victory at Omdurman, they outflanked Marchand at Fashoda.

France burned with chagrin. Yet Kitchener and Marchand got on well together. Only a year later, their two countries settled their longstanding differences on North Africa and Egypt, on West Africa and the Siamese frontier. The watershed between the Congo and the Nile was taken as the dividing line between British and French spheres of influence in Africa. In such collaboration lay the germ of the *Entente Cordiale*. British primacy in Egypt was upheld. Morocco was partitioned between France and Spain, the latter already a West African power.

Having been dislodged from Fashoda, Marchand continued eastwards to the Red Sea at Djibuti. His original objective had been to reach Ethiopia. There the Russians were as busy as they are today. The Orthodox Church of Holy Russia desired understanding and even, however perversely, union with the Ethiopian monophysites; and St. Petersburg backed France against Britain and Italy in East Africa.

A Russian expedition of 1889 ended at Sagallo, on the Somali coast, in a diplomatically embarrassing clash with the French, who, for reasons uncertain, fired upon their Russian allies. After that date, a number of Russian military expeditions penetrated Ethiopia. Russian arms were sold in quantity to the Emperor Menelik; Russian advisers were attached to his forces. This may well have led to the Ethiopian victory over the Italians at Adowa in 1896. An Ethiopian mission to Russia in the previous year was enthusiastically welcomed, and a year after the battle, twelve young Ethiopians were sent to St. Petersburg to be educated at their Emperor's expense.

The most prominent Russian adventurer in Ethiopia, Nicolas Leontiev, acquired a position of vast influence at the court of the Emperor Menelik, and, in 1899, led an expedition of conquest into equatorial Ethiopia, with the Emperor's authority. The Emperor, however, became alarmed at the risk of a clash with the British in Kenya, and indignant when it was revealed that Leontiev had raised funds in Belgium on the strength of gold concessions allegedly granted to him by the Emperor. As a result, he was dismissed, but various other Russian officers continued to serve with the Ethiopian forces.

Ethiopia preserved the independence of centuries until the Italian occupation of 1935.

47

Liberia, colonised from 1821 by American Negro freed-men, whose descendants still form that country's ruling caste, persisted as a republic, with a constitution modelled on that of the United States.

Otherwise, the establishment of effective French, Spanish and Italian control of North Africa in the early years of the twentieth century completed the partition of the continent.

CHAPTER VI

Brief Empire

In the space of sixty years, from the discovery of the
Niger basin (1826–32) to Stanley's last African journey in
1887, Africa was opened up to the ambitions and aspirations of Europeans. The Evangelical movement and the
quest for trade and knowledge played an equal part in this
process. The Arab slave trade aroused horror throughout
Europe. Few Europeans doubted or disputed the merits of
Western civilisation. Thus political intervention became the
means of implementing a policy of philanthropy—and when
partition became inevitable, it was just as inevitable that
each interested power should stake its claim to a share in
the division of the continent.

The partition itself took only twenty years to complete
(1879–98). Professor C. F. Carrington gives a just ver-
dict upon what some historians have denounced as disgrace-
ful :

> "If ever any historical sequence was inevitable—economic-
> ally determined—it was this. In the age of steam-power,
> cheap manufactures, rising population, surplus capital and
> liberal philanthropy, nothing could have prevented these
> various forces from impinging upon Africa : the question
> was whether the impact should be disorderly or orderly.
> According to the Marxist myth the financiers, seeking an
> outlet for surplus capital, were the 'governors of the engine'
> which advanced through Africa. But it is difficult to trace
> their direct influence upon the expenditure in blood and
> treasure which the French lavished in the Sahara Desert, or

upon Bismarck's tortuous diplomacy, or upon the creation of the South African protectorates. It would of course be absurd to deny that speculative finance played a dominant part in the making of Rhodesia and the Congo, but it is a jaundiced view that cannot see what Rhodesia also owes to the ideals of Livingstone and what the Congo owes to those later Belgian administrators, who have righted the wrong done by King Leopold."[1]

The Europeans shed less blood in the partition of Africa than the Americans did in their wars against the Indian nations of the United States. Nor did either World War harm Africa as much as Europe or Asia. But, though the colonial powers co-operated to suppress the slave trade, they otherwise worked almost in isolation. How much more might have been achieved if the expansion of Europe in Africa had been accomplished by a unified body of Christian states instead of as a scramble for spheres of influence.

Neither in colonisation, however, or in decolonisation, did the Europeans have any common philosophy. Their *imperium* was brief; its story, apart from the Portuguese epic, was that of a single century. Old men, who had witnessed Lugard's conquest of Northern Nigeria, lived to see the Union Jack hauled down.

In the years before the First World War, the colonial powers, untroubled by nationalist revolt, were able to stamp out many of the embers of traditional tribal resistance and to exploit or neglect the estates which they had marked out with scant regard for ethnic identity or sentiment.

As far as Britain was concerned, her principal aims in Africa were defensive and strategic. Before the beginning of the twentieth century, she did little to organise or develop

[1] *The British Overseas: Exploits of a Nation of Shopkeepers*, O.U.P. 1950.

her African territories. The Indian Empire was her first priority.

The British moreover lacked imperialist philosophy until the late nineteenth century. The attitude of many of her politicians was typified by Gladstone, who said in a speech at Leeds in 1881 : "And so, gentlemen, I say, while we are opposed to Imperialism, we are devoted to the Empire." Until the last decade of the century, many saw the empire as a political gambit. To many Liberals, again following Gladstone, it was "Dizzy's suit of imperial spangles".

Only with Joseph Chamberlain's Tariff Reform League, which captivated elements of the working class, with the publication of such works as Seely's *Expansion of England*, and the work of Milner and his *Kindergarten*, did a coherent imperialist philosophy emerge. Both Milner and the Liberal Imperialist, Lord Rosebery, made of empire a larger patriotism.

In a changed world after the First World War, however, Britain, in common with the other colonial powers, found that she had to justify her stewardship, especially after taking over responsibility for former German colonies under League of Nations Mandate. Europe was on the defensive throughout Africa. She suffered, as General Smuts told the Imperial Conference in London in 1921, "from an exhaustion which is the most appalling fact of history". Lugard who, like Lyautey in Morocco, had encouraged a policy of indirect rule through the Emirs, proclaimed in 1922 in his *Dual Mandate in British Tropical Africa* that :

"Europe is in Africa for the material benefit of her own industrial classes, of the native races in their progress to a higher plane; that the benefit can be made reciprocal, and it is the aim and desire of civilised administration to fulfil this dual mandate."

In France, Albert Sarraut, as Minister for Colonies, declared that the obligation of the metropolitan power was not merely to govern justly, but to advance the governed. "Peaceful penetration", bringing Algeria into contiguity with Senegal, and expansion to the Ivory Coast, the Congo and the shores of Lake Chad, furthered the grand scheme of *La France d'Outremer* unified, centralised, and embracing half the African continent. France's "colonial children" had fought in the trenches of Champagne. "France," General Mangin exulted, "is a nation of a hundred million." All her multi-various subjects would be French, or become French—French without distinction of race, religion, colour or culture. French would be their common, noble, language. Arab children in Algeria would learn in their standardised history books of their Gallic descent! *Instruire la masse, et dégager l'élite* was the precept of General Gallieni, of Madagascar, Senegambia, the Sudan—and the Marne. As early as 1898, city dwellers of all races in Senegal were given full French citizenship together with parliamentary representation in Paris.

France was fortunate in her African *élite*. Dodds, the conqueror of Dahomey, was a Negro. So were Diagne and Candace who served on the Council of Ministers in Paris. Mayran won the *Prix Goncourt*. Felix Eboué was to become a distinguished Governor-General, *le premier résistant de la France*.

Such a policy of assimilation proved harder to implement in the *Maghreb* than in Black Africa. Here Islam was a barrier. The soldier-saint, Père Charles de Foucauld, predicted that, unless the Muslims of French North Africa were converted to Christianity, a dissatisfied intellectual *élite* would arise comparable with that of the Turkey of Enver

Pasha, who had led the revolt of the Young Turks against the Sultanate. Outwardly French, this *élite* would be :

> "French neither in mind or heart, lacking all Muslim faith, but keeping the name of it to be able to influence the masses, who remain ignorant of us. . . . In the long run the *élite* will use Islam as a lever to raise the masses against us. The population is now thirty million : thanks to peace it will double in fifty years. It will have railways, all the plant of civilisation, and will have been trained by us to the use of our arms. If we have not made Frenchmen of these peoples they will drive us out. The only way for them to become French is by becoming Christian."

Economically, France was protectionist in Africa. Lord Salisbury had written bitterly :

> "Wherever Great Britain has undertaken the task of developing and civilising the interior, French trade profits equally with that of Great Britain, but the tendency of French arrangements is to obtain exclusive privileges for French commerce."

Imperial preference was circumscribed, not only by the continued British belief in the virtues of Free Trade, but by the two Congo Basin Treaties. The Berlin Act provided for freedom of navigation and freedom of trade on the Congo and the Niger, and prohibited customs duties. The Brussels Act, on the other hand, allowed customs duties to be levied, provided that they did not discriminate in favour of one or more signatories of the Act against the remainder. The Anglo-Egyptian Sudan, Kenya, Uganda, Nyasaland, Zanzibar and parts of Northern Rhodesia were thus prevented from granting preference to any fellow country in the Empire—a restriction which was to complicate even the establishment of the Central African Federation. In the same way, the Class B Mandated Territories, which Britain and

53

Belgium had taken over from Germany, also fell within the area covered by these treaties. Moreover the Anglo-Dutch Convention of 1871 laid down that the Gold Coast should not give preference to Imperial over Dutch goods.

Belgium redeemed a reputation tarnished by the scandals of the Congo Free State by establishing an admirable administration and educational system. Lord Hailey, in his masterly *African Survey*, wrote of the Belgian determination that the strongest possible contrast should be presented to the history of the Free State under Leopold II. As in French Africa, there was no official colour bar. Nor was there in Italian territory.

The British however were culturally less self-confident and racially more exclusive. Britain's preoccupation with India and the aspirations of that country's native educated class left less time and energy for the implementation of her African responsibilities.

The two Ormsby-Gore Reports, for East Africa in 1924, and for West Africa in 1926, called for the promotion of medical, educational and agricultural services. When Leo Amery, a disciple of Joseph Chamberlain, served at the Colonial Office, he called together the Governors from British Africa and instituted a policy of subsidising, inspecting and improving the Christian mission schools. In 1923, the Conservative administration decided, to the disapproval of Asian as well as European settlers, that in Kenya, as in Uganda, "the interests of the African natives must be paramount, and if the interests of the immigration races should conflict . . . the former should prevail". The White Paper in which this doctrine is enshrined went on to say that "H.M. Government regard themselves as exercising a trust on behalf of the African population, and they are unable to delegate or to share that trust".

54

Amery, Lord Delamere, and others, urged the formation of the East African territories into a single Dominion. But when the Labour Colonial Secretary, Lord Passfield, formerly Sidney Webb, reaffirmed the policy as laid down in 1923, and warned the settlers not to expect an advance towards self-government, they withdrew their support for Closer Union. In that year, Southern Rhodesia obtained responsible government under the Crown.

Until the Second World War, and afterwards, the colonial powers, though they differed in methods and approach, were at one in seeing no end to their tutelage, and the need for it. But the education they had introduced, and indeed the war service of many Africans, encouraged the imitation in Africa of the nationalist principles which for so long had dominated Europe.

Ethiopianism expressed through Negro churches a reaction against the Christianity preached by Europeans. The roots of such a reaction go back almost to the first days of Empire. Mohammed bin Abdulla Hassan fought a *jihad* against Britain in Somaliland in 1901. John Chilembwe's bloody yet pathetic revolt in Nyasaland in 1915, or Abd-el-Krim's tenacious guerrilla struggle against France and Spain in the Moroccan mountains in the 1920's, were also revulsion against the alien forces, spiritual and economic, that were loosening traditional ties and dissolving tribal discipline.

European empire ended the old pattern of tribal warfare. Many customary orgies were put down. The black arts were proscribed if not suppressed. At the same time, Christian orthodoxy did not sufficiently compensate primitive Africans for the boredom and frustration that accompanied an alien Imperial peace. It was of a Kikuyu house, "empty, swept and garnished", that the old devils, and new, took possession. The plantations and cash economy of the whites co-existed with the age-old subsistence farming and shifting pastoral life of the natives. It did not end it. Indeed, the British Colonial Office tried to preserve traditional peasant economies. Nevertheless, migrant labour was sucked out of the tribal society and the subsistence economy, to the modern society and cash economy, with their social and spiritual restlessness.

But for a while peace and the rule of law reigned—two blessings which the Imperial powers provided, and which were taken for granted until the agony of their loss.

Chapter VII

Anti-Colonialism

The entry of the United States of America into both world
wars made eventual victory over Germany and her allies
certain. The Great War of 1914–1918 transformed the
United States into a world power, able to exert her influence over the proud nations of Europe. But the Senate
expressed the will of the American people, when, by declining to accept the consequences of Woodrow Wilson's
foreign policy, it refused to bid for that world supremacy
which Max Weber, for one, pronounced to be "as inevitable
as that of Rome in the ancient world after the Punic Wars".
The American people were still responsive to Jefferson's
isolationist warnings against entangling alliances.

Except in the Pacific, then, as now, of even greater con-
cern to America than the Atlantic, the United States withdrew into isolation without having guaranteed the Versailles
peace settlement. It did not join the League of Nations,
for which President Wilson had been enthusiastic. Nor did
Washington accept any mandate for ex-German colonial
possessions. The triumph of the Republican candidate,
Harding, in the Presidential elections of 1920, confirmed
American withdrawal into the wings of the world stage, and
anger over unpaid war debts strengthened isolationist feeling.

After the Second World War, it was different. The
United States became pre-eminent in both military and
material power and in economic potential. This time there

could be no retreat from greatness. Points of economic advantage and strategic advantage were not relinquished. On the 1st June, 1942, Sumner Welles connected the very outbreak of a Second World War with the failure of his country to follow through an international collaboration after World War One.

In his book, *As I Saw It*, Elliot Roosevelt quoted the President, Franklin Delano Roosevelt, as telling Churchill that he :

> "can't believe that we can fight a war against a Fascist slavery, and at the same time not work to free people from all over the world from a backward colonial policy."

This view was shared by F.D.R.'s Republican opponent in the Presidential election of 1940, Wendell Wilkie, who, in his book, *One World*, followed the President in calling in the New World to redress the balance of the Old.

Roosevelt saw himself as the universal propagator of the ideals of the Revolution of 1776, and as early as the 16th November, 1917, he was mentioned in Colonel House's *Diary* as lecturing the British Government, when he visited London "telling them, among other things, how to govern Egypt".

A U.S. State Department paper, No. 2812, published in 1947, recalled the colonial origins of the American people themselves, who "have traditionally fostered a liberal attitude toward dependent territories and toward the aspirations of non-self-governing peoples". In fact this "liberal attitude" was of recent date. An earlier attitude was that of "manifest destiny" in fulfilment of which President Polk had carried Old Glory to the further seas. Secretary Seward had proclaimed under Lincoln an American Empire which should stretch from the Arctic to Tierra del Fuego. Franklin

D. Roosevelt's cousin, Theodore, had believed in speaking softly, but also in carrying a big stick. The Philippines were "incorporated" in the Union, the Panama Canal built, and the Canal Zone occupied in what might well be described as a subtle equivalent of the Bombardment of Alexandria. Rudyard Kipling adjured the Americans to "take up the White Man's burden".

For a few years, Republican policy was proudly Imperialist. Washington did not refuse or disdain Joseph Chamberlain's offer of British friendship. Teddy Roosevelt admired the British Empire and shot big game in Africa. Like Cecil Rhodes, he believed in Anglo-American alliance. Speaking at the Guildhall, in June 1910, he said of the Anglo-Egyptian Sudan:

> "I do not believe any other country has made such astonishing progress as it has made under British rule."

In the same speech, he expressed very different views on Egypt to those of his cousin:

> ". . . speaking as an American and a Radical, I say that Great Britain has given Egypt her best government it has had for two thousand years."

Woodrow Wilson, however, recoiled from empire, despite the Mexican Expedition of 1915, and Franklin D. Roosevelt preferred the role of "good neighbour" to that of imperial master. To him and his Secretary of State, Cordell Hull, the British Empire was particularly suspect. Its preferential trading arrangements were objectionable. To remove this discrimination became a condition of war-time and post-war loans, lease-lend, and aid under the Marshall Plan.

For the new super-powers after the Second World War, anti-colonialism did not begin at home. But both applied their righteous, or self-righteous, doctrine to the contracting empires of Europe. The U.S.S.R. straddled half of Europe herself, and the United States made strategic annexations in the Pacific. Anti-colonialism however was one piece of common ground between Liberal America and Leninist Russia. General Eisenhower held that not only his country-men, but the Russians were "free of the stigma of colonial empire-building by force". President Roosevelt professed himself convinced that Stalin was not an imperialist; unlike the British, who "would take land anywhere in the world even if it were only a rock or sandbar".[1]

In fact, the British were in full retreat from their colonial responsibilities. By the end of 1947, the King was no longer King-Emperor. London could no longer use the Indian Army to defend the oil fields of Arabia and Iraq. The Palestine Mandate was abandoned. The Americans moved in on Abadan and urged the British to withdraw from Egypt.

The standards of world power were now set by the two vast anti-imperialist empires. How was war-weary Britain to keep her footing? In a speech to the Empire Parliamentary Association on the 25th November, 1943, General Smuts had urged her to "strengthen her European position", by enlisting the nations of continental Western Europe in the next worldwide British system. Europe and the Commonwealth, Europe and "Europe Overseas" needed each other.

General de Gaulle spoke to the Free French Consultative Committee in Algiers on the 18th March, 1944, of *"un groupement occidentale prolongé par l'Afrique et dont la Manche, le Rhin, la Mediterranée seraient comme les artères"*; and Sir Stafford Cripps told the Conference of African Colonial Governors in November, 1947 :

[1] Stettinius, Edward R. Jr.: *Roosevelt and the Russians.*

60

"Further development of African resources is of the same crucial importance to the rehabilitation and strengthening of Western Europe as the restoration of European productive power is to the future prosperity and progress of Africa."

In 1947, the Treaty of Dunkirk was signed, largely due to the persistence of the British Ambassador in Paris, Duff Cooper. This was designed to cement the Anglo-French alliance for fifty years. In 1948, the two powers were joined by the Benelux countries, under the terms of the Brussels Treaty, to form the Western Union. The British Foreign Secretary, Ernest Bevin, spoke of the wider implications of the event :

"I am not concerned only with Europe as a geographical conception. Europe has extended its influence throughout the world, and we have to look further afield. In the first place we turn our eyes to Africa, where great responsibilities are shared with us by South Africa, France, Belgium and Portugal. . . . The organisation of Western Europe must be economically supported. That involves the closest possible collaboration with the Commonwealth and with overseas territories, not only British, but French, Dutch, Belgian and Portuguese.

"These overseas territories are largely primary producers and their standard of life is expanding rapidly and is capable of great development. They have raw materials, food and resources which can be turned to very great common advantage, both to the people of the territories themselves, to Europe and to the world as a whole."

The Hague Conference of the European Movement declared :

"The European Union must, of course, include in its orbit the extensions, dependencies and associated territories of all the European powers in Africa and elsewhere, and must preserve the existing constitutional ties which unite them."

"Eurafrica" was an idea that embraced Right and Left alike. In Britain its propagators included Sir Oswald Mosley and Sir Stafford Cripps. The President of the Board of Trade, Harold Wilson, said in the House of Commons on the 6th July, 1948, that he agreed that :

> "The development of so far undeveloped territories in Africa and elsewhere can do more good than any other single thing to redress the world balance of payments."

Later, Raymond Cartier put it bluntly in an article in *Paris-Match* in 1953 :

> *"Sans l'Afrique, l'Europe n'est qu'une petite presqu' île surpeuplée et dépendante. C'est une raison précise et suffisante pour ne pas s'en dessaisir, même s'il faut lutter pour la garder."*

But there had been long since African thinkers and doers with other ideas. By the turn of the twentieth century, African intellectuals were vehemently questioning the European assumption of innate Negroid inferiority, and taking pride in their ancestral past. They could quote *De la litteràture des nègres*, by the Abbé Gregoire who, during the French Revolution, had moved for the abolition of slavery in the French colonies and had asserted the intellectual abilities of the black races. The suppression of the African slave trade and the arrival of European empire and education produced an African *élite* which included Honorio Barreto, Governor of Guinè, the freedman Ajayi Crowther who became the first Anglican Bishop of Nigeria, and the mulatto Dodds, of Dahomey.

Africans began to write their own history. In Nigeria, the Rev. Samuel Johnson compiled *A History of the Yorubas* in 1908. In the Gold Coast, Casely Hayford demanded in his book, *Ethiopia Unbound*, published in 1911, the establishment of a systematic scheme of study for African history. His claim that "Africa was the cradle of the world's philosophies and the nursing mother of her religions", would be echoed by many writers, English and French speaking, and by Kwame Nkrumah. Sir Apologo Kagwa, a Roman Catholic, knighted by Queen Victoria, wrote at length of the traditional institutions and folklore of the Kingdom of Buganda, which he served as Prime Minister for thirty-seven years.

The articulate expression of pride in the past and the culture of Africa was bound to find political outlet. Pan-Africanism, a movement which had originated among the descendants of Negro slaves in the West Indies and in the United States, inspired a sense of Negro destiny, a longing for Negro solidarity. These emotional feelings became bound up with the political demand of "Africa for the Africans".

In 1858, a Negro, Edward Blyden, who had been born in the Dutch West Indies, was ordained as a Presbyterian minister. At a time when many anthropologists were convinced of the Negro's congenital inferiority, Blyden travelled through both Europe and Africa, refuting this theory. He held that it was more African for the Negro to reach Christianity through Islam, and that in any event, evangelisation could never be accomplished by alien missionaries. In 1891, Blyden lectured at Lagos on the "Return of the Exiles of the West African Church", and it was there that the United Native African Church was founded. The Negro must have his independent churches, for the adoption of foreign manners and customs led to quenching the spirit. Too many missionaries were indeed unable to express the Gospel in other than European terms. Polygamy was a massive stumbling block to conversion to orthodox Christianity.

This, however, the proliferating independent churches of West Africa often permitted. Their appeal was Africanist, but not political. Black leaders and intellectuals in South Africa, such as Solomon T. Plaatje, D. D. T. Jabaru, M. S. Molema and the eminent novelist Thomas Mofolo, a pupil of the French Protestant pastors in Basutoland, as well as the Zulu Chief Lutuli, sprang from the older European streams of Christianity.

The political Pan-African movement was publicly launched by a Trinidad lawyer, H. Sylvester Williams, who convened a congress in London to protest against British colonial policy in Africa. The Congress was attended by the American Negro, Dr. W. S. B. DuBois, who was to succeed Williams as the leading Pan-Africanist.

A contemporary, and vivid, advocate of Negro rights was Marcus A. Garvey, whose Universal Negro Improvement Association stood for world-wide Negro solidarity and the idea of "Back to Africa". Half a century before Kwame Nkrumah, Garvey too aspired to the Presidency of the "United States of Africa".

DuBois had devoted himself primarily to the struggle for inter-racial equality in the United States. Then, he too turned to Africa. In 1919, he took advantage of the discussions at the Versailles Peace Conference on the future of the German colonies in Africa to open a campaign for a universal union of black peoples which would fight for better conditions and eventual political independence. Between 1919 and 1927 he convened four Pan-African Congresses in Europe and in America, at which were asserted the rights of Africans to land in Africa, and to participate in the administration of their countries, "in so far as their development permitted".

In the 1930's there arrived on the scene the American

educated West Indian, George Padmore, who was the first editor of *The Negro Worker*. This Communist broadsheet, published in Hamburg, was the organ of the Trade Union of Negro Workers, and Padmore's task was to stir up unrest among Negro seafarers. Among those employed on the paper was Jomo Kenyatta. In 1934, Padmore rejected Communism—his book is entitled *Pan-Africanism or Communism*—and three years later he and Kenyatta moved to London to found, with other Pan-Africanists, the International African Services Bureau, which published the periodical *Pan-Africa*. In 1938 Kenyatta denounced the dispossession of the Kikuyu by British settlers in his book *Facing Mount Kenya* and praised primitive tribal lore not excluding female circumcision. The Ibo Dr. Nnamdi Azikiwe, author of *Renascent Africa*, exulted in the medieval empires of West Africa, as did Charles de Graft Johnson in his *African Glory*.

Dr. Azikiwe published in 1943, through the International African Services Bureau, a memorandum which demanded an end to British colonialism. In the following year members of the Bureau founded the Pan-African Federation which stood for the independence and unity of Black Africa. It was during this formative period that George Padmore met Kwame Nkrumah and became his friend and adviser.

Padmore, Nkrumah and Kenyatta combined to turn into political action the shadowy philosophy of *négritude* and "African personality". The ideas of Du Bois and Garvey also influenced Modebo Keita, the former director of *Les Ballets Africains*, and J. B. Danquah, who chose the name "Ghana" for the Gold Coast. These were respectively *francophone* and English-speaking exponents of the cult of black identity, which found extravagant expression in the insistence of Kobina Parkes and of another English-speaking Ghanaian, Raphael Armattoe, on the blackness of God. Congolese messianic sects believed that Jesus Christ suffered only for the whites.

A sense of *négritude* pervaded the last great Pan-African rally held outside Africa. This was staged at Manchester in 1945. The next Congress of importance would not take place until 1958, in Accra. Unlike those earlier assemblies which had been dominated by Negro exiles and *élites* of the Caribbean, the U.S.A. and Europe, together with a few intellectuals from colonial Africa, the Manchester Congress reflected what Padmore described as "a militant leadership closely linked with the popular movements in the homelands". Prominent at Manchester were Peter Abrahams from South Africa, Joe Appiah of the Gold Coast, Chief Akintola of Nigeria and, from Sierre Leone, T. A. Wallace-Johnson. The Congress condemned colonisation for the poverty and balkanisation of Africa.

Négritude however is pre-eminently the preserve of intellectuals of French-speaking Africa. The idea itself was defined by the Senegalese philosopher and poet, Léopold Sédar Senghor, as

"the whole complex of civilised values—cultural, economic and political—which characterise the black peoples, or, more precisely, the Negro African world . . . the sense of communion, the gift of myth-making."

Senghor is a Catholic, albeit over-influenced by Teilhard de Chardin. He volunteered for war service and was taken prisoner by the Germans. In Paris in 1947, with Alioune and Diop, he set up the magazine *Prèsence Africaine* as a counter to French cultural domination. Gidé, Camus and Sartre were among the contributors. In 1956, the magazine organised the first Congress of African Artists and Writers.

Senghor asked God's forgiveness for :

"France who preaches the straight path but takes the crooked one herself,
Who invites me to her table yet tells me to bring my own bread,
Who gives to me with the right hand but takes half away again with the left."

He was torn in two directions and was not alone among African thinkers in his ambivalence. It was no clear cut question that he posed between white and black, inferior and superior, but between different states of mind—the one African and instinctive, the other European and discursive. *Négritude* was the black branch of what English-speaking Africans called "African personality". There was another, Arabo-Berber.

Senghor's cult was of the "universal". Thomas Diop, for example, was narrower and more bitter :

"The White man killed my father; my father was proud.
The White man raped my mother; my mother was beautiful.
The White man beat my brother working beneath the sun on the road; my brother was strong."

Egypt was the cradle of civilisation : Europe lied about the ancient Egyptians. They were black Africans who became paler by miscegenation.

This dubious aspect of *négritude* gave it bad marks in Moscow. Until three years ago, Soviet Africanists commented favourably on it. Senegal was the first French-speaking African state to recognise the U.S.S.R. and to exchange Ambassadors with the Kremlin. President Senghor was expected in Russia, but in the event his visit was indefinitely postponed. In 1969 Soviet propaganda attacked Senghor's

African Socialism[2] as both "bourgeois" and "Francophil", and supporting "racist theories" that implied African inferiority. Fanon, in *Les Damnés de la Terre*, and the South African Ezekiel Mphahlele, have condemned *négritude* as narcissistic, and at the first Pan-African Cultural Congress in Algiers Marxists and their allies pronounced it dead. With fine distinction and some classical erudition they wanted the concept replaced by that of "Melanism".

After European decolonisation Pan-Africanism became the ideology of the unsuccessful empire-builder, Nkrumah, just as Pan-Arabism was pressed into service by Nasser. Despite the O.A.U. and a number of groupings and "Communities", this idea is at present an aspiration as unreal as the continental design of the fictitious Reverend John Laputa in John Buchan's romance, *Prester John*.

[2] Theories of "African (or Arab, or Islamic) Socialism" reflect anticolonial ideology and lack of private or domestic capital for development. "African Socialism" is distinguished by Marxists from what they choose to call "Scientific Socialism". The Russians have become less sanguine about the prospects of their version of Socialism being built in one leap in Africa. Cf. Professor Mirsky, *New Times*, September, 1969 on Africa's "weak, amorphous social structures and the prevailing of ethnic tribal relations over class consciousness". He did however see some evidence of "progress" in the "non-capitalism" of some states, such as Zambia and Tanzania, with its Arusha Manifesto, and before his overthrow by the military *coup* of General Amin in January, 1971, Dr. Milton Obote had his Common Man's Charter for Uganda.

The downfall of President Keita of Mali in 1968 left Guinea the only state in West Africa pursuing "Scientific Socialism". Indeed, President Sekou Touré has described the Soviet Union as a "reactionary force" and China as the source of Guineans' "revolutionary consciousness". However, Egypt bears witness that Communist powers can dominate states that even persecute Marxism.

Chapter VIII

Decolonisation

Invasion, occupation and liberation from the Axis powers drained from Europe the blood and vitality spared by the Great War a generation earlier. Two super-powers, each selectively anti-colonial, emerged triumphant from the struggle; the one almost unscathed, the other devastated, but enlarged by half a continent, yielded to it by Western folly. The weakness of the European colonial powers, the hostility of both Liberalism and the Left to their imperialism, and the ideology, idealism and ambitions of the super-powers encouraged the demands of educated Africans for the independence that India and Indonesia, for example, had won from Britain and the Netherlands.

In 1955, an Afro-Asian Conference was opened at Bandung, in Indonesia, by President Sukarno. Twenty-six countries were represented by revolutionary movements in exile. They included Algeria, Zanzibar, Senegal, the Cameroons, Uganda, Kenya, Chad and the three Somaliland territories of Britain, France and Italy.

A dominant voice at Bandung was that of Chou En-lai, whose oratory had a potent effect upon a number of African and Asian leaders, including Nehru and Nasser. The Soviet Union was heir to the Russia-in-Asia of Tsardom; yet its claim to be regarded as an Asian power was rejected and Moscow was not invited to send a delegation. Only now did the West realise that the People's Republic of China had special aspirations and ambitions for the colonial and the ex-colonial world. Even the Soviet Union had only lately granted that Peking would be no pliant lieutenant in its own designs. But although Bandung foreshadowed the future Sino-Soviet schism, it gave no comfort to the colonial powers. It condemned all colonialism and imperialism and promised full support for those struggling to liberate themselves from it.

West Africa, with its advanced intelligentsia and a history of long contact with the West, led in the decolonisation race. When the Second World War ended, consumer goods were in short supply and returned ex-servicemen full of expectations. Danquah brought Nkrumah home from England. In 1948, a boycott of European traders was declared in the Gold Coast. Rioting broke out. The two-year-old constitution had, for the first time in Colonial Africa, granted an African majority in the Legislative Council. The enquiry into the causes of the riots led to further constitutional reform. But Nkrumah led the demand for "self-government now".

The scramble out of Africa had begun. A Labour Government imprisoned and then released Nkrumah. The Conservatives installed him as Prime Minister and Harold Macmillan welcomed him to the Commonwealth Conference in 1957. Even today, after his overthrow, the name of Nkrumah still adorns the ranks of the Privy Council. A Labour Commonwealth Secretary deposed Seretse Khama of Bechuanaland and a Conservative successor removed the Kabaka of Buganda.

One positive, though belated, step was taken by the Conservatives. In 1953, they formed the Federation of Rhodesia and Nyasaland, the Central African Federation. Basing its constitution on the principle of multi-racial partnership, they hoped to interpose a multi-racial Dominion between

South Africa and the emerging independent states of the North. But in territories where there were no white settlers —and even in Kenya where there were—the precedent set by the Gold Coast nullified the fine phrases about co-operation between the European powers in Africa. Instead of co-ordinating an orderly withdrawal, these powers leap-frogged over each other in the wholesale abdication of African responsibilities, and the United States, upon which they had become dependent, gave them no encouragement to stay. Indeed, the Declaration of Washington, proclaimed jointly by President Eisenhower and the British Prime Minister, Sir Anthony Eden, in February, 1956, conceded to the United States a right to a say in the promotion of self-government in British dependencies.

"Because of the belief that the state should exist for the benefit of the individual and not the individual for the benefit of the state, we uphold the basic right of peoples to government of their own choice. During the past ten and more years . . . 600 million men and women in nearly a score of lands have, with our support and assistance, have attained nationhood. Many millions more are being helped surely and steadily towards self-government. Thus, the reality and effectiveness of what we have done is a proof of our sincerity."

Nineteen hundred and sixty was called "the Year of Africa". It witnessed the independence of the Federation of Nigeria and of the Somali Republic, the former within the Commonwealth, the latter without it. The Somali Republic embraces the former British Somaliland Protectorate and the Italian colony administered by Britain from 1941 until the end of 1950 and by Italy under U.N. resolution until 1960. French Somaliland is now the Territory of Afar and Issa. Sierra Leone and Tanganyika gained Commonwealth status in 1961. Zanzibar was liberated to geno-

71

cidal revolution in 1963. The Gambia became independent in 1965, and Basutoland as Lesotho in 1966, followed by Bechuanaland as Botswana, and the Kingdom of Swaziland in 1967.

The zeal for British, and European, decolonisation, shown by President Eisenhower in 1956, was not without its economic significance. In 1962, a trust company in the United States published this advertisement :

"The new-found independence of so many new African nations means many new opportunities for American business men. In the colonial era, African trade and investment were controlled in Europe. But now many African countries are actively seeking dealings with Americans, to end their dependence on Europe."

But where Americans replaced Europeans, Russians could not be expected to stand idly by. The dislodgement of Britain from Egypt opened Africa to Soviet influence and subversion. In 1952, General Neguib and a cabal of young nationalist officers seized power and forced King Farouk to abdicate. In 1953, the Sudan Agreement conferred self-government leading to self-determination—not that either right was conceded to the Negro, and Christian, Southerners. Secessionist resistance to the administration in Khartoum led in 1963–4 to the mutilation, torture, imprisonment and expulsion of Catholic priests and people. Hundreds of Christians were reported to have been killed in the Anglican Cathedral in Juba. Thousands of Christian refugees fled into Uganda and the Congo.

Meanwhile in 1954, the Suez Agreement, following on the heels of the Sudan Agreement, ended British military occupation of the Canal Zone and control of the Nile Valley.

Gamal Abdel Nasser, who overthrew the genial Neguib,

72

was as responsive to the Soviet as to the American Ambassador. His tactics, since widely imitated, were to play East against West and blackmail both. This handsome, modern Saladin dreamed of a new Egyptian advance up the Nile. But despite the unremitting propaganda of Cairo Radio to much of black Africa the Arab north meant slavery and the rhinoceros-hide *kiboko*. In Nigeria, the Yoruba Chief Obabemi Awolowo warned the Negro peoples of Africa against a collaboration with Nasser which would eventually reduce them to the role of satellites. They would, in fact, have become the satellites of a satellite. The *Rais* in Cairo sold his country's cotton in exchange for arms from the Soviet *bloc*. He sold his country too. An Enver Pasha rather than an Ataturk, he chose adventure rather than development, notwithstanding his imperialism was the imperialism of a vassal. Red Flag and Green Flag advanced together, for Russia became progressively as much the master of Egypt as ever Britain was in the time of Cromer or Killearn.

President Banda of Malawi wisely summed up the position in July, 1968:

"To what tribe does Nasser belong? Is he a Zulu, a Kikuyu, an Ashanti? The Arabs are no more indigenous Africans than the Europeans. As I am speaking here, Arabs are murdering Africans in the Sudan. South Africa may send Africans to prison, but I have never had any African from South Africa telling me that his village has been bombed to ashes. I have had three Sudanese come to me in tears because their village has been bombed."

As an attempt to restore European influence, the Suez expedition of 1956 failed disastrously. The American attitude was decisive. Mr. Nixon, then Vice-President, hailed it as a "declaration of independence that has had an electrifying effect throughout the coloured world". The future President continued:

"Because we took the position we did (against British and French intervention in Egypt), the people of Africa and Asia know now that we walk with them as moral equals, that we do not have one standard of law for the West and one for the East. They know, too, that the United States has no illusions about the White Man's Burden or White Supremacy.

"The Suez affair marked a turning point in history because the United States deliberately deserted the colonial powers which had been its traditional friends. We pledged our support to nations formerly held as colonies by the major powers."

The super-powers now glowered at each other in a region where they had been hitherto separated by the British and French.

For the French, the short-lived *entente* with Israel,[1] which Abba Eban described as animated by a "special chivalry", together with the Suez enterprise, were part of the defence of Algeria against a nationalist guerrilla movement, sustained by outside powers. France's task was already complicated by the independence of Morocco and Tunisia. "French North Africa," General Georges Catroux wrote in 1949,

"was caught in a wind of emancipation, coming at once from the East and from across the Atlantic, coming also from the depths of naturally intractable Berber souls and from the religious intolerance of Islam."[2]

This was the fulfilment of the prophecies of the Sahara's soldier-saint, Père de Foucauld.

[1] Encircled by Arab States open to Soviet penetration and denied the use of the Suez Canal, the State of Israel stretched out a cautious hand to the Lion of Judah and the Southern Sudanese. It also extended technical and military advice and formed joint undertakings all over Africa. In 1962 President Sauko of the Central African Republic visited Israel and said: "You have not tried to create us in your image . . . you have conquered black Africa."

[2] *Dans la Bataille de la Mediterranée, op. cit.*

In 1955, Moroccan revolt forced the restoration of the Sultan, whom Marshal Juin had deported. In 1956, the Sultanate received full sovereignty, and it was not long before it recovered the International Zone of Tangier, together with the territory protected by Spain, other than Ceuta and Melilla which remain Spanish. Tunisia received her independence soon afterwards. The Bey of Tunis was deposed in 1957, and Habib Bourguiba became the no less autocratic President of the one-party Tunisian Republic.

The case of Algeria was different. Unlike the protected monarchies of Tunisia and Morocco, she was a French province. Her European population, the first generation of which had settled in the country in the 1830's, numbered between one and two million. Algeria was French before Nice. The Arab leader, Ferhat Abbas, found no Algerian nation "on this soil which has been French for a thousand years". These words are taken from a book he wrote in 1937. *La France, c'est moi*. "There has never yet been," said Camus, "an Algerian nation."

The Algerian departments were within the area covered by the North Atlantic Treaty. But France's so-called allies were a broken reed. An article by Jacques Bainville in *L'Action Française* of the 10th July, 1925, makes curious reading today. He wrote of the possible threat to the French Empire :

"Either we shall be driven out of Morocco, or we shall remain there. If we were driven out, it would be the sign of such decadence that all North Africa would soon follow suit. Algiers would once again become a nest of pirates and Barbary submarines *(des sous-marins barbaresques)* taking the place of the old felucca would not be long in reappearing off the coasts of Europe. These suppositions are not as fantastic as they seem. If Europe begins to retreat in Africa and Asia, one cannot conceive how rapidly the rout would become general."

In October 1957, M. Michel Debré was saying :

"If Bizerta, Algiers and Mers-el-Kebir stop being French, France will have a Mediterranean frontier to defend in twenty years as in ancient times, only it will be more difficult then."

When de Gaulle changed—as he did—Debré changed too.

Restored to power in 1958, General de Gaulle rejected the dream of *Algerie française* that inspired those who brought him back from retirement. The speeches he made and the letters he wrote, refute the assertion that he dissembled about his commitment to that cause. For Charles de Gaulle, as for Winston Churchill, consistency was not part of greatness. He belonged moreover to the continental, not the colonial, school of military thought. Like the young Disraeli, the young de Gaulle disputed the value of overseas possessions. "What real and lasting profit," he asked in 1934, "can be had by such annexations?" His eyes were fastened on the blue line of the Vosges, not dazzled by the heat-haze of the *bled* (desert). To him, the Niger and the Congo were nothing to the Rhine and the Danube, and he grudged Algeria the troops needed for his latter-day "Confederation of the Rhine". So the General strove for an honourable peace and the formation of a Franco-Algerian association which, with the Sahara and its oil and mineral potential, would be linked to France in a united *Maghreb*. The remains of Lyautey were brought back from his beloved Morocco to rest in the *Invalides*, Pantheon of continental wars.

Algeria, abandoned by France, fed on American grain and was armed by the East. The fatal incarceration of Moise Tshombe in 1967 was worthy of Bainville's "nest of pirates".

Jacques Soustelle attributed France's surrender to a selfish bourgeois preoccupation with *les weekends et les vacances* and to racism. Unlike the Portuguese, but like the British, the French were unwilling to associate with Africans, Arabs, Berbers, or even the Maltese, Spanish and Greek *colons* of the *Maghreb*. As Rome incorporated Gaul, France should have incorporated Africa. Instead, the bourgeois bowed before the idol of decolonisation and the pressures of mercantile capitalism. For Soustelle, true decolonisation would have come, not from surrender to the "fascism" of the F.L.N., but from incorporation, with equal rights and advantages for all, without any distinction of class, creed, or colour. This course was rejected. Black Africa was allowed to be converted into a *poussière* (dustheap) of petty dictatorships.

Yet as recently as 1944, the Brazzaville Conference had looked forward to an extended common citizenship throughout the French Empire. Félix Eboué, as Governor-General of French Equatorial Africa, formulated principles for what was to be called the French Union. These were enshrined in the Constitution of the Fourth Republic :

"France constitutes with the peoples overseas a Union founded upon equality of rights and duties, without any distinction due to race or religion."

Sarraut himself became President of the Council of the French Union. But as a formal structure, it soon collapsed. The British in West Africa were offering a swifter advance to independence, and French West Africa could not lag behind.

In 1956, a Socialist government in Paris included Félix Houphouet-Boigny of the Ivory Coast. He drafted a *loi-cadre*, providing for a measure of territorial self-government. In 1958, President de Gaulle offered to every territory in

77

both French West Africa and French Equatorial Africa, the choice between complete and separate independence, or autonomy within a French Community, which would deal with foreign policy, defence and other common functions. French Guinea, under Ahmed Sekou Touré, alone rebuffed the General, and declared for complete separation. In 1959, Senegal and the French Sudan asked for complete independence within the French Community as the short-lived Federation of Mali.

Thus, despite their historical, philosophical and temperamental differences, both French and British had arrived at a similar destination. The Community became almost as loose an association of states as the Commonwealth. Indeed, Senghor used the phrase Commonwealth *à la française*, and, in 1965, spoke of a "Commonwealth *francophone*". This was to include not merely the countries of the *Organisation Commune Africaine et Malgache* which in that year replaced the *Union Africaine et Malgache de Co-operation Economique*,[3] and other former French colonies like Guinea, Mali and Mauritania, but also *nos amis du Maghreb*. Such an idea of a linguistic and cultural unity has since been carried beyond Europe and Africa.

Not to be outdone by Senegal and the Sudan, the territories within the influence of Houphouet-Boigny's *Rassemblement Démocratique Africain*, namely the Ivory Coast, Niger, Dahomey and Upper Volta, obtained their independence outside the Community, while aiming at achieving a new understanding with France. In 1959 the four republics set up a *Conseil de l'Entente*.

[3] *Organisation Commune Africaine et Malgache* has fourteen members: Cameroon, Central African Republic, Chad, Congo-Brazzaville, Congo-Kinshasa, Dahomey, Gabon, Ivory Coast, Malagasy Republic, Niger, Rwanda, Senegal, Togo and Upper Volta. Mauritius, a Commonwealth realm, later joined the Organisation.

Economically, French Africa remained even more dependent than Commonwealth Africa[4] on European markets and on European aid-programmes. The fourteen members of O.C.A.M. all became associated with the European Economic Community, under the Yaoundé Convention, as did Mali and Mauritania as well as Burundi and the Somali Republic. Treaty and other economic arrangements between the countries of the *Maghreb* and France and her European partners, continue to mark the inescapable connection between the two sides of the Mediterranean.

Senghor wrote of the commercial, financial and also parliamentary association between French-speaking Black Africa and the E.E.C. :

> "Free peoples had decided to take their destiny into their own hands. . . . For us, association signifies the setting on foot of new economic relationships which are not characterised by domination."

Only Guinea, which cut off all its ties with France, did not profit by such an association. Under the rule of one Marxist party and the unstable Sekou Touré, the country knew increasing impoverishment and oppression, punctuated by real or stimulated revolt and staged treason trials the last of which, in February, 1971 was followed by further executions and led to condemnation from many of the leading statesmen of the French-speaking group of African states.

In 1968 André Malraux, as Minister of Culture, addressed the General Assembly of the *Association Internationale des parlementaires francophone* at Versailles :

> "I believe that in collaboration with these nations, the culture of France is playing the same part that was formerly played by the culture of ancient Greece. This is one of the

[4] The East African members of the Commonwealth and Nigeria have negotiated an Association Agreement with the E.E.C.

most challenging adventures of the mind that our century
has known, that of the mingling of African culture with that
of world civilisation. With its sculpture, its dancing and its
music, Africa has become aware of her own potential. We
know that . . . ancestry is not fetishism, and we have found
that these fundamental values which President Senghor
proclaims . . . as *négritude*, are mainly expressed by French-
speaking Africans. We are helping to create a true Afro-
Latin cultural community."

The idea of such a community was advanced by Senghor,
taken up by Bourguiba and brought to fruition by President Diori Hamani of Niger in whose capital, Niamey, the
Agence de Co-operation Culturelle et Technique was set
up.

Like the Commonwealth, it has a Canadian Secretary
General in M. Jean-Marc Leger. But despite this new, and
wider, body, the Commonwealth *francophone* has fewer
formal institutions than has the Commonwealth. Above all,
it avoids general conferences and therefore the posturing
and pontificating of rulers fearful of being outflanked on the
Left which have converted the formerly intimate meetings
of Commonwealth Premiers into a wrangling "mini-U.N.".

France's relations with Africa are for the most part bi-
lateral. Under and since General de Gaulle, M. Jacques
Foccart sits at the centre of a web of influence and information radiating from the Presidency of the Republic to its
African replicas. The wheel has turned full circle from older
ideas of assimilation and organic union to that of co-operat-
ing sovereignties.

A large question mark hangs like a halo behind the heads
of the rising generation of potential rulers; for the present,
however, France's grip on the imagination and sympathies
of the French African *élite* exceeds Britain's hold on her
erstwhile pupils. *Francophone* statesmen have their villas

in France; which leaders of Commonwealth Africa own manor-houses in England? South Africa retains proportionately more French advisers. In Chad the Foreign Legion and other units have been engaged in upholding President François Tombalbaye against the disaffected nomads of Tibesti and the *Front de Liberation nationale du Tchad (Frolina)*.[5]

To generalise, the educated French African is more steeped in French culture than is the intellectual of Commonwealth Africa in that of England. The teaching of French began earlier in *francophone* Africa than did the teaching of English in the Commonwealth territories. Many French soldiers and administrators have found more affinity with Negro than with Arab, which could hardly be said of their British opposite numbers. French attitudes have been freer of the colour sense and guilt-induced obsequiousness with which Leftist Britain has approached the least helpful rulers of Commonwealth Africa.

France profited by a Labour Government's adherence to a total U.N. ban on the export of arms to South Africa. Her sale of submarines and aircraft have not prejudiced the intimacy of her African connexions. The British Prime Minister was treated at the 1971 Commonwealth Conference in Singapore to prefabricated African tirades against the Conservative policy of resuming sales for maritime defence, whereas not long after Mr. Heath's return to London from Singapore, President Pompidou set out with the benignity and acclaim of a welcome uncle for a tour of Mauritania, Senegal, the Ivory Coast, Cameroons and Gabon, and stated, in Dakar, France's intention of continuing to supply arms to the South African Defence Force.

[5] This might be likened to a Biafra-in-reverse.

Chapter IX

East West Cockpit

There were few Communists in the African independence movements, but their propaganda was impeccably anti-colonialist. Moscow boasted of having threatened the imperialists with their rockets into evacuating Suez; and Soviet influence appeared to have been potently exerted to extract independence from the colonial powers. The myth of Russian backwardness before 1917 and of dynamic industrialisation since commended the socialist system to African leaders, impatient to construct a modern economy with exiguous resources of skill and capital. The more the colonialists and capitalists abused Communism the more the less percipient African nationalists took it at its propaganda value.

So whether in collaboration, or in competition, Soviet Russia and Communist China trod hard upon the heels of retreating Europeans. Africans, particularly from the South and most notably from the Portuguese Provinces, were sent not only to Moscow for "academic" courses in Marxism, but were given military training both at the Simperopol camp in the Crimea and at the Moscow Intelligence School. Fortunately, the Communists have often overplayed their hand, swallowing too readily socialistic slogans of nationalist parties. Their behaviour has revealed ignorance of Africa and shown arrogance towards Africans, who have found Communist operators as cold and calculating as any capitalist exploiter or colonialist oppressor. Africans are emotional people—and an atheistic dialectic carries little appeal. Students back from the Soviet *bloc* have complained of racism and African students have rioted collectively in Red Square.

Despite their advantages, then, the Communists bungled their early ventures into Africa and alienated much of the *élite*. Pro-Communist régimes in Ghana and Mali were short-lived, although Soviet relations with Mali remained friendly after the fall of Modibo Keita in 1968.

Under Nasser, Cairo became an outpost of Communist subversion.[1] The Afro-Asian People's Solidarity Organisation was set up there in 1958 with an Egyptian Secretary-General. Control rested with the U.A.R., the U.S.S.R. and the Chinese People's Republic.

According to Major-General Jan Sejna, who defected during Dubcek's "Prague spring" of 1968, and had been concerned with arms deals with Nasser, the Czechoslovak Chief of Staff, General Rytir, said that "the prospect . . . of roping the Egyptian and Syrian intelligence service into the Communist net" would "help us penetrate the Arabs and even other coloured people. A Negro will always trust an Arab more than he does a white man" [*sic*][2]. The Eritrean Liberation Front, which is a sharp thorn in the imperial side of Ethiopia, has received training with Palestinian guerrilla groups and Soviet and Eastern European arms through Arab states. Thus Moscow hopes to avoid embarrassing its diplomacy with African states.

After five hundred years China, too, is back in Africa. In the fifteenth century, naval squadrons of the Emperor touched at Mogadishu and, in all probability, Aden. It is

[1] It should be remembered that Stalin sought Soviet entry into the Mediterranean and Africa in 1945 when the U.S.S.R. applied for U.N. trusteeship over Tripolitania.
[2] *Sunday Telegraph*, 7.2.71.

believed that Chinese crews wintered on the East African coast somewhere south of Sofala, where they waited for the western monsoon to blow them homeward. In a way, Mao preceded Moscow in the African theatre of subversive operations. The Chinese gave the F.L.N. active support in Algeria and trained guerrilla fighters for insurrection in Camerum. Colonel Kan Mai, from the Chinese Embassy in Brazzaville, served with the Mulelists who terrorised Stanleyville. From the time of the Bandung Conference Chinese diplomacy was active in both Arab and African countries. In 1961 Peking was represented at an A.A.P.S.O. meeting in Conakry.[3] The Embassy at Dar-es-Salaam became not a "gateway of peace" but a Communist gateway to Eastern Africa.

In 1963 Chou En-lai toured the U.A.R., Algeria, Morocco, Tunisia, Ghana, Guinea, Mali, Sudan, Ethiopia, Somalia as well as Albania, Peking's main ideological ally. The Chinese Premier exuded altruism. He recited the five principles plus those added at Bandung. He enunciated five more to guide Chinese policy in Africa. In Ghana he denounced Western trade and aid as selfish and enumerated eight principles to govern the giving of Chinese aid. A meeting with Nkrumah produced five more. As a result, he adjudged that "revolutionary prospects were excellent in Africa".

The Sino-Soviet schism meant that an "anti-pope" in the East disputed with the collegial "papacy" in Moscow for primacy over the Marxist orthodox and for the patronage of the Third World, that Achilles heel of capitalism. From Hunan in 1927 Mao Tse-tung brought the strategy of encircling the cities from the countryside. Mao Tse-tung's second in command, Marshal Lin-Piao, adapted this theory

[3] A.A.P.S.O.: Afro-Asian People's Solidarity Organisation.

to the Third World and stated that the encirclement of the industrialised "city" (Europe and North America) would be accomplished from the "countryside" of Africa and Latin America.

> "Taking the entire globe, if North America and Western Europe can be called the 'cities of the world', then Asia, Africa and Latin America constitute the 'rural areas of the world'. Since World War II the proletarian revolution has for various reasons been temporarily held back in the North American and West European capitalist cities, while the people's revolutionary movement in Asia, Africa and Latin America has been growing vigorously. . . . In the final analysis, the whole cause of world revolution hinges on the revolutionary struggles of the Asian, African and Latin American peoples."

In 1966 the author was shown a copy of the Marshal's booklet amongst other Chinese literature found on terrorists from north of the Zambesi intercepted near Sinoia in Rhodesia.

The quarrel between Moscow and Peking disrupted the A.A.P.S.O. conferences at Moshi (Tanganyika) in 1963 and at Winneba (Ghana) in 1965. The Organisation split. The Chinese impugned the "revisionism" of Russia; the U.S.S.R., retaliated with charges of "demagogy", "ultra-nationalism" and "racism".

> "The Chinese cadres (*Isvetzia* complained on the 16th July, 1964) who, practically claiming that they are the leading Marxists in the world . . . are consciously or unconsciously impressing on the Afro-Asian peoples that they are superior to the white race."

From President Nkrumah, as from President Nasser, Russia hoped much. Nasser aimed at mastery in the three circles of his *Philosophy of the Revolution*, Arab, African, Muslim. Nkrumah saw himself, despite the inferiority of

85

Ghanaian to Nigerian resources, as the federator of Pan-Africa. In 1958 he held a conference at Accra. Among those who attended was Patrice Lumumba from the Belgian Congo and Holden Roberto. The latter was born in the Portuguese Congo in the north of Angola but had been educated and employed as a clerk in Belgian territory, where he had lived from childhood.

Lumumba was rated a "moderate". He believed that

"it would be impossible, in the relatively near future, to grant political rights to people who were unfit to use them, to dull-witted illiterates; that would be to put dangerous weapons in the hands of children."

At Accra however he became an "activist". He marked his return to Leopoldville by instigating a riot. In Brussels, Ministers lost their nerve. After a Round Table Conference plans for the independence of the Congo were advanced to June, 1960. Anarchy supervened and the tribal divisions the Belgians had disciplined broke out in an ugly rash of massacre and separatism.

The Katanga province under President Moisé Tshombe seceded from chaos. This was more than a manoeuvre of the Anglo-Belgian *Union Minière*. Tshombe was the son-in-law of the paramount chief of the formerly powerful Lunda, an imperial tribe also represented in Northern Rhodesia. There was thus logic, as well as opportunity, in Sir Roy Welensky's notion of linking Katanga with the Federation of which he was Prime Minister. The rich Katanga mines are contiguous with the Zambian Copperbelt. Of Katanga's considerable white population, only 60 per cent were Belgian. Swahili, little spoken in the hot and humid provinces down country, was the *lingua franca* of Katanga's temperate uplands. Leopoldville (now Kinshasa) was as far from the Katangan capital, Elisabethville (now Lubumbashi) as

86

Paris from Prague. Katanga itself was twice the size of Western Germany.

The mutiny of the *Force Publique*, the breakdown of order, and Belgian airborne intervention to save life prompted in July, 1960 the Congo's appeal for United Nations assistance. By ruse and brutal force U.N. forces first penetrated Katanga and then suppressed its secession. A world organisation dedicated to peace and self-determination waged war to deny it. Once again the U.S.A., which largely financed the Congo adventure, the U.S.S.R. and the Afro-Asian *bloc* were united against European interests. For Tshombe's crime was his friendship with Europeans and his co-operation with the *Union Minière* to preserve the basis of Katanga's prosperity. In 1958, a year and a half before independence, Elisabethville was the only one of the Belgian Congo's seven cities to be governed by a municipality with an African majority. Inter-racial partnership was a fact in Katanga before white and black found themselves fighting shoulder to shoulder in the streets of Elisabethville, turned by U.N. into a Budapest.

Dr. Albert Schweitzer, who had devoted half a century to Africa at his hospital at Lambaréné in Gabon, found it

"incomprehensible that a foreign Power is found making war on Katanga in order to force her to pay taxes to another Congolese State. How can a civilised country undertake such a thing? Still more strange, the United Nations has associated itself with this foreign country, thereby losing the respect it enjoyed in the world. It is not the mission of the United Nations to make war . . . the independence of Katanga derives from the fact that the empire of the Belgian Congo no longer exists."

Tshombe later became for a space Prime Minister of the Congo with which he was always ready to link Katanga in loose confederation. His exile and his death in captivity in Algiers was discreditable to the régime of President Boumedienne, but more so to the supine governments of the West and in particular that of Great Britain from under whose flag the great African was kidnapped. Tshombe is dead; but, as he himself said in 1961, "the United Nations died in Katanga".

Georges Bidault, leader in more than one "resistance", wrote :

"It was U.N. pressure which forced the Belgian Congo to remain a single state, although that country boasts two hundred and seventy-five different tribes and can hardly be called a nation or a people. Yet Ambassador Stevenson declared without hesitation that the secession of Katanga was as unthinkable as the secession of an American state. It really is impossible to understand why people feel so strongly on this point. After all, Katanga could easily have been made Portuguese by Serpa Pinto or English by Cecil Rhodes. It so happened that Leopold II and Stanley took it over and made it Belgian; but it is no more Congolese than Rhodesian or Angolese. And how could the U.N. approve of Algeria's secession when it condemned Elizabethville? Perhaps I ought not to repeat one explanation : that there was too much petrol and copper on the world market and that the best way to check Katanga's copper production was to refuse to allow Elizabethville to go independent while the best way to slow down the Sahara's oil output was to give Algeria its independence. But I really ought not to repeat this slanderous accusation; I am positive those who made it forgot what a fraternal and disinterested world we live in."[4]

It was from the independent, inchoate Congo that Angola was invaded. Portugal has been at war in Africa ever since. Early in 1960, the "Year of Africa", the year of Congolese liberation to chaos, disruption and civil war,

[4] *Resistance:* the political biography of Georges Bidault. Marianne Sinclair tr. Weidenfeld & Nicolson.

the American Committee on Africa inaccurately asserted the existence of disturbances in Angola. In the succeeding months Communist and Afro-Asian agencies concerted their designs.

In October Mr. Krushchev appeared in New York to proclaim *urbi et orbi* his support for anti-colonialism.[5] His demagogy was vulgar but the Africans found it persuasive, and its success may be measured by the disastrous manner in which first Harold Macmillan, then President Kennedy proceeded to outbid the Soviet Union in anti-colonialism.

Afro-Asian representatives at the United Nations alleged a "threat to peace" in Angola as they and others later invented a threat to peace in Rhodesia. A resolution on these lines was supported in the Security Council by both Krushchev's Russia and Kennedy's America. Galvão's murderous piracy was intended as prelude to an uprising in Angola. What in fact occurred were co-ordinated and simultaneous incursions of Angolan expatriates organised by Holden Roberto. They committed such atrocities on a peaceful population, mostly black, that one must conclude that their perpetrators were acting under drugs and inflamed by witchcraft. Holden and colleagues of the U.P.A.[6] organisation later boasted to *Le Monde "avec un large sourire"* of running the owner of a sawmill and his family "lengthwise through the buzzer".

Settler reprisals were terrible, but ended with the arrival of Portuguese regulars in this almost ungarrisoned province the size of the Iberian Peninsula plus France and Germany. The trouble in Angola was as local as the intermittent frontier operations in Britain's former Indian Empire. U.P.A. was at loggerheads with the rival M.P.L.A.[7]

[5] Livermore, H. V.: *A New History of Portugal*, C.U.P. 1966.

[6] *União das Populacôes de Angola.*

[7] *Movimento Popola de Libertaçao de Angola.*

89

and, as in Mozambique, invaded from Tanzania in 1964, disaffection was confined to one or two tribes straddling the Portuguese frontiers. Profiting, as against Belgium, by the legend of the past, Portugal's enemies used U.N. for virulent propaganda. Nkrumah's Ghana brought charges of forced labour against Portugal who was acquitted of them by the International Labour Organisation. But the Communist powers and some of the African governments were less concerned with the aspirations and welfare of black Africans than with the subversion of Southern Africa and European interests throughout the continent.

At the Tricontinental Conference at Havana in 1966 the Afro-Asian Solidarity Organisation became an Afro-Asian-Latin American Solidarity Organisation and Cuban officers, doctors and technicians have appeared with the revolutionary forces operating since 1962 against Portuguese Guinea. Unrebuked, indeed encouraged, by organs of the U.N., and drawing funds and even arms from West as well as East, internationally organised terrorism has also been mounted against South Africa (which withdrew from the Commonwealth in 1961) and her territory of South-West Africa. As for Rhodesia, hostile arms were being run across the Zambesi before the Unilateral (or illegal, as Whitehall preferred) Declaration of Independence.

Chapter X

Some African Realities

We speak of "African nationalism". But what is nationalism in a continent where there has been no nation as we understand it? Nigeria, for example, was, in the estimation of Chief Obafemi Awolowo, "not a nation but a geographical expression".

And what is meant by African? Tribes within the confines of a single African state may differ more profoundly than the Scandinavian or Slav from the Latin peoples of Europe. An African state may include not merely a number of tribes, but distinct racial groups. In Kenya, for instance, one distinguishes the Hamitic Somali of the northern frontiers from the Nilotic Luo and the dominant Kikuyu who are Bantu. The significance of tribalism in Uganda was brought out by Major-General (afterwards General) Idi Amin at his first press conference after his seizure of the reins from Dr. Milton Obote in February, 1971. The General explained that the deposed President had planned to hand military power over to the Acholi and Lango tribesmen of the north, and to disarm soldiers from tribes less favourable to him.

In Kenya loyalty to President Kenyatta runs strong across the tribal lines. Nevertheless, many Luo resent the privileged position of the Kikuyu, who despise them as "fish eaters". When the explosive Mr. Oginga Odinga, who has been suspected of sympathy with Peking, parted political company with the President, he took with him most of his Luo adherents. To restore confidence, Kenyatta promoted some Luos. Yet fears persist of a permanent Kikuyu predominance.

According to the former Foreign Minister of Portugal, Dr. Franco Nogueira :

"The tragedy of Africa . . . is that just now reality . . . consists of incessant *coups-d'état*, the extermination of one tribe by another, civil wars, repression, economic ruin, a return to tribal rule and the domination of the new countries by neo-colonialist forces concerned with interests rather than ideals."

The imperial powers drew boundaries with more regard for their own bargains and convenience than for ethnic identity. Kwame Nkrumah denounced the cynicism with which tribes and even villages were parcelled-out. The Togo-Dahomey frontier, among others, is a tribal crisscross.

Nor did the retiring colonial rulers bequeath national entities that could command higher loyalties than those of the tribe. Black excellencies with many honorific titles banquet in elaborately guarded State Houses.[1] Black ministers and permanent secretaries sit at the desks of white predecessors. Theirs now are the tinsel and trappings of sovereignty, the sweetness of deference and the shining, pennanted cars that have given their name to such new and privileged tribes as the "Wa-Benzi".[2] It is true that the arts of self-rule must be learnt by practising them. On the other hand, certain conditions and attainments are needful, if the self-teaching is to succeed. No one, however gifted, can organise a modern state if no unifying allegiance

[1] What a contrast between the security at State House, Lusaka, and the single police sentry outside the Prime Minister's suburban residence at Salisbury !

[2] From the ubiquitous Mercedes-Benz.

proves stronger than the fissiparous and insistent demands of kith and clan.

Indeed, the European task in Africa was left unfulfilled. Anti-colonialism, with its Eastern and Western virus, blighted the young buds of a promising growth. Political sovereignty was hastily conferred on many African territories lacking a trained *élite* and devoid of the sociological basis for independence. In December, 1956, Julius Nyerere told a questioner on the Fourth Committee of the U.N. General Assembly that he thought that "Tanganyika should be independent in about ten years". In the event, independence was conferred in 1961. That many African leaders have achieved so much is a tribute to their qualities, rather than a credit to the European powers who made insufficient preparation for independence. The late Tom Mboya was an assistant sanitary inspector, Dr. Kenneth Kaunda a teacher, Mr. Joshua Nkomo, of Southern Rhodesia, a social welfare worker, and President Mobutu, of the former Belgian Congo, a prison book-keeper with the rank of sergeant.

Not that the European powers alone are to be blamed for the troubles brought by independence. Some African leaders have themselves realised this. Mr. Tom Okelo-Odongo, a former Assistant Minister of Finance in Kenya, said :

"It is often the foreign imperialist that is blamed for our economic stagnation. We explain our political instability and social turmoil by attributing them to foreign machinations. The African is the major source of his own afflictions."

Wole Soyinka, who was imprisoned in Nigeria for his support of Biafra, accused his African fellow-writers of failing to anticipate "the movement towards chaos in modern Africa".

In March, 1966, President Sekou Touré of Guiné said

93

that President Kasavubu of the Democratic Republic of the Congo "told me during our last meeting in Accra that more than a million and a half people had been killed in the Congo". Forty-five thousand Europeans fled in the first three weeks of independence. Two hundred and ninety-one white women are reported to have been raped. But the blacks were, as elsewhere, the most grievous sufferers. It is said that many Congolese plaintively asked: "When will this Independence end?" No one will ever be able to count the victims of the conflicts in Burundi, the Southern Sudan and Nigeria, once Britain's African showpiece. Freedom has there meant freedom to rob and be robbed, rape and be raped, or to die slowly of starvation. Yet we are sometimes told, with a shrug of the shoulders, that Africa's agonies of independence are "growing pains".

The full horror has been concealed or censored from the world. Why? Because it was too frightful to report and to photograph? This seems unlikely; sadism is part of the stuff of our daily mass entertainment. Is it then the influence in the news media of those who have made of the so-called Third World a kind of collective "Noble Savage"? Or is it that our rulers, and those who preceded them, do not wish to be reminded that premature decolonisation was a betrayal of all obligations save those of commercial and financial interest?

The Portuguese have not been guilty of such dereliction. Their resolute conduct stands as a rebuke to the shameful inconsistency of their so-called allies. Is that why the latter are so eager to prove Portugal wrong in their obduracy and adjure them, in terms of sorrowful counsel or of vilification, to follow their Gadarene descent? But then Portugal, whether in Africa, Asia or Europe, is an authoritarian state, but a state ruled by law and through representative institutions. In this and in other respects Portugal is the European power closest to African mentality.

Democracy, as known in Europe, has failed to take root in Africa. Free speech, a free press, and the concept of "loyal opposition" are out of keeping with African outlook and realities. From time immemorial, where chieftaincy has obtained, the chief's decision has been preceded by lengthy discussion, but, once made, the decision must be unquestioningly accepted. Parliamentary institutions, as known at Westminster, exist in Africa, but only where there is a European population resolute enough and sufficiently numerous to predominate until the formation of a strong Black African *élite* and middle class, are they likely to survive.

The norm in independent Africa is the one party state. "One man, one vote", has meant, and could only mean, one vote for one party or one man. "Quite frankly," said Sir Roy Welensky in a characteristically breezy comment, "when you look around at the bloody mess that exists in Africa today, you cannot make a case for one man, one vote."

Ali A. Mazuri says in his book, *Towards a Pax Africana: A Study of Ideology and Ambition* :

"The language of African nationalism in recent times has tended to suggest that the central aspiration was liberty, indivisible or not. Single word slogans like *Uhuru, Kwacha* and 'Free-Dom' have emphasised this. So has the understandable conceptual framework which makes 'anticolonialism' a demand primarily for 'liberation'—and proceeds from there to the precarious conclusion that the basic motivation behind African nationalism is a desire for 'freedom'. That African freedom is immensely important to the African nationalists is, of course, beyond doubt. But it is not to be hastily assumed that the average African really shares Lord Acton's conception of liberty, not as a means to a higher political end but as itself the highest political end.

The average African does not rate liberty even in the sense of 'independence' so high. Instead . . . nationalism in Africa is still more egalitarian than libertarian . . . the slave needs his freedom to be the equal of all men, as well as to exercise it."

Whether it be Dr. Franco Nogueira or the late Franz Fanon, the theme is disenchantment. In *Les Damnés de la Terre* Fanon complains that decolonisation in Black Africa has produced disenfranchised slaves, dependent still on metropolitan paymasters. Pornography and alcohol corrupt the young. The national liberation party becomes a private bureaucracy for the advancement of public men, who, though black, are really white. The police are still there. Only their pigmentation has changed. African rulers savour the delights of the city and free foreign travel. They desert the countryside and abandon a peasantry hungry for land and even food. The people, Fanon urges, must not be treated thus. They must be understood and must take part in the struggle to increase agricultural production and overcome illiteracy.

Independence has not cured poverty. Much of the soil of Africa is losing its fertility. Erosion spreads, agricultural methods remain backwards, the soil is deliberately and wastefully burnt. The *Maghreb* relies upon gifts of food from North America. Nigeria imports basic foodstuffs to the extent of 10 per cent of her total imports—Ghana nearer 20 per cent.

Malnutrition is rife, even allowing for the lesser number of calories required for healthy tropical existence. Protein is short. In some communities, custom bans some nutritious foods, including those that supply nitrogen. Malaria is declining—especially in Portuguese territories—but not bilharzia. Tuberculosis is still rife.

The expectancy of life is only 40 in Zambia and Lesotho and 27 in Mali. In white South Africa, it is 65. According to figures published by U.N.E.S.C.O., the average wage in Black Africa is £10 *per annum*. In Rhodesia, it is £125.

In education, as in other fields of social welfare, South Africa and Rhodesia lead the way. In 1964, the U.N.E.S.C.O. Report of the Conference of African States in Abidjan recorded that 91·5 per cent of Rhodesian children between five and fourteen were at school. Of these, 627,808 were African and 35,770 European. The figures since have shown a proportionate increase. Nigeria had only 40·8 per cent of such children in school—this was before the carnage of Biafra—Tanganyika 29 per cent, the Sudan 15·9, Mali 7·7, and Ethiopia 5 per cent. One in six of Rhodesians were in school. The British figure was one in five. Literacy in Malawi and Zambia reached 40–60 per cent, but nowhere else in Black Africa was it so high. In Upper Volta, literacy was as low as 5 per cent.

Sir Eric Ashby's Commission, which enquired into education in Nigeria, reported that within ten years 130,000 more secondary school places would be needed, 5,000 more teachers and a sevenfold increase in University capacity. These statistics must remain statistics until Nigeria has recovered from the havoc of war.

Early in 1969, the United Nations Economic Commission for Africa recorded its disappointment with African progress in the period 1960–66, despite many encouraging developments. Expatriate advisers and technicians would be needed for at least the next decade. Levels of development were generally low. Only in Rhodesia and the United Arab Republic did manufacturing industries contribute more than 20 per cent to the gross national product in 1966.

Many of the new states of Africa became so corrupt with independence that Stanislav Andreski[3] described their system of government as "Kleptocracy". In his pamphlet, *Vive le Président*, the French-speaking Cameroonian, Daniel Ewanda, assailed the vanity and incompetence of African heads of state. There is a great gulf fixed between the "haves" —the politicians and bureaucrats and the "have-nots"—the peasants and semi-educated unemployed. In no Black African country has a true middle class emerged to keep the balance. Corruption is an endemic and insidious disease which, combined with inefficiency, becomes intolerable until assassination or *coup d'état* brings other men to power.

Emmanuel J. Hevi was an anti-colonial Ghanaian who studied in Moscow. He wrote :[4]

> "It is very distressing to see the way some African governments fritter away in prestige items the little money they are able to borrow. Some of our ambassadors ride in much more luxurious automobiles than the ambassadors of the countries that grant us aid; their banquets are more sumptuous, their residences more palatial. Our ministers and our politicians pay themselves more princely salaries than either our state coffers allow or our countries' living standards warrant. And what do we want with imposing stadia and half-empty hotels that cannot pay their way? What is desirable is aid that helps to make us less dependent."

These are but a few of the problems facing independent Africa that can no longer be concealed by an excess of slogan-shouting. African leaders, faced too by a soaring birthrate, must look to their own responsibility, for their own people, before they turn southward on a hopeless "crusade".

[3] *The African Predicament*, Michael Joseph 1968.
[4] *The Dragon's Entrance: The Chinese Communists and Africa.* Pall Mall Press 1967.

Unfortunately, abuse of their governments and national policy by African spokesmen, the expropriation of their assets and the expulsion of their nationals have hardened many European hearts against aid, and many European minds against the investment of risk capital in Africa.

Chapter XI

Raise the Double Standard High!

After the referendum of 1922 and formal annexation to His Majesty's Dominions, the principle was accepted that "the Parliament at Westminster does not legislate for Southern Rhodesia except at her request". Her Prime Minister was invited to Commonwealth Conferences. In another referendum, that of 1961, the Southern Rhodesia electorate accepted the "Sandys" constitution providing for eventual majority rule as Africans gained the necessary educational and property qualifications. Many of the whites voted for it, but reluctantly and on the understanding that under this constitution Southern Rhodesia would attain full autonomy within the Federation, or, if that were dissolved, full independence within the Commonwealth.

They knew what had happened elsewhere. They had seen and succoured refugees from the Congo. Their Prime Ministers had suffered disillusionment in London with those they had fondly thought of as gentlemen of the old school. The black nationalist leaders had endorsed in Britain, then repudiated in Southern Rhodesia, the new constitution which opened a wide door to their advancement. Their confrères to the North had shown that a more advanced constitution could be extracted in London almost before the ink had dried on its predecessor. The rival parties Z.A.P.U.[1] and Z.A.N.U.[2] scourged township and reserve with petrol bomb and bicycle chain, their terrorism being

[1] Zimbabwe African People's Union led by Mr. Joshua Nkomo.
[2] Zimbabwe African National Union led by the Rev. Mr. Sithole.

directed at least as much against each other's supporters as against the white Government. Places of worship and learning were destroyed, innocent Africans murdered or mutilated. These factors contributed to the triumph of the Rhodesian Front led by Mr. Ian Smith, who was excluded from the Commonwealth Conference to appease some of its less helpful members, and to its acceptance by all races, notably the African victims of political gangsterism and those who walked in fear of it.

That freedom from fear, and freedom to stay alive, is even more important than freedom to vote was explained to the then Commonwealth Secretary, Mr. Arthur Bottomley, with typical Bantu dignity and eloquence by the Chiefs gathered in *Indaba* at Domboshawa on the 2nd March, 1965:

> "It is obvious to us, Sir, that however much truth we can speak today, it is not the intention of you, our honoured guest, to be satisfied with what you know to be the truth. If we take you to the graves of these people who have been killed, you will not be satisfied that they have been killed by these nationalists. If we show you the graves of the children of our people who have been killed by these people, you will not be satisfied. If we show you the churches, the dip tanks and our schools that have been damaged by these people, you will not be satisfied. . . . Sir, if it is your wish to hand over to the nationalists, well, we cannot stop you; but all we can say is that if you do the time will come when the person who is about to die will point his finger at you."

After the signing of the Declaration of Independence beneath the Queen's portrait—its concluding words were "God save the Queen"[3]—Mr. Smith broadcast to the nation. He saw no future for Rhodesia "if we are to remain

[3] Washington toasted King George after the Declaration of Independence. Both leaders had fought for the Crown, both were tobacco farmers—except that Ian Smith's black labourers were free and Washington's were slaves.

drifting in this constitutional twilight". U.D.I. was the product of despair of a negotiated independence.

November 11th was the day chosen for the bloodless break. The British Prime Minister spoke at Westminster. Rhodesia would be excluded from Commonwealth preference and advantages. There would be a total ban on purchases of Rhodesian tobacco and sugar. But, said Mr. Harold Wilson, "our purpose is not punitive". The question of Rhodesia moreover remained a "domestic issue". But under Left Wing and African pressure he proceeded to severer measures that were in some cases vindictive although ineffectual. Oil sanctions, at first precluded, led to the blockade of Beira—but not of Lourenço Marques. The latter port in Moçambique was important to South Africa and Mr. Wilson was determined that there should be no "confrontation" with South Africa who supported the Rhodesian pound and, with Portugal, refused co-operation with the policy of sanctions and ignored the mandate of the U.N. Security Council. Had Mr. Wilson's advisers forgotten South Africa when at Lagos, at the first Commonwealth Prime Ministers' Conference to be held outside London, he assured his colleagues that the rebellion would be suppressed "in a matter of weeks rather than months"? At the end of 1966 however Rhodesia was still defiant in growing unity and increasing self-sufficiency and the British Government requested the U.N. Security Council to impose mandatory sanctions.

To them the special legalism applied to Rhodesia alone must seem abstract indeed. Nevertheless the High Court at Salisbury, which Mr. Wilson enjoined to continue the administration of justice despite U.D.I., is agreed that what Whitehall terms an "illegal régime" is the Government of Rhodesia. There was disagreement in the Appellate

Division which heard the constitutional test case brought on appeal by two detainees[4] whether that Government is *de jure* or *de facto*. The High Court has also held that the 1962 Constitution was incompatible with colonial status. However that may be, even if Southern Rhodesia is a rebellious colony, such international law authorities as Oppenheim and Brierly assert that if the "mother-state" fails to subdue revolt the "colony" ought to be recognised as a "state". In recognising so many revolutionary régimes in Africa, British Governments have laid stress on whether the new rulers exercise "effective control". Rhodesia's worst enemies could not dispute that her Government is most effectively in control.

Two parleys between the two Prime Ministers, in H.M.S. *Tiger* at the beginning of December, 1966, and in H.M.S. *Fearless* nearly two years later, were abortive. Sanctions continued to benefit some of Britain's trading competitors who entered a market where she had enjoyed almost a monopoly. Fervent royalists whose loyalty to Crown and Commonwealth had been written in the blood of two world wars and in subsequent service outside Rhodesia were converted into resentful republicans. More British than the British, they became anti-British. The last Union Jack to be officially flown by an African Government was lowered. Those to whom South Africa's ideology was most repugnant had succeeded in enlarging its influence in Rhodesia at Britain's expense. Rhodesia is no more an extension of England. She is as much a part of Southern Africa as is Canada of North America and, like Canada, Rhodesia will find that she must assert her national identity against Mother Country and great southern neighbour alike.

[4] There have been fewer persons detained and restricted than under Sir Edgar Whitehead's "legal" State of Emergency before U.D.I.

The Rhodesian Declaration of Independence was in part modelled on the American. This accused George III, among other crimes, of exciting against the settlers "the merciless Indian Savages". A "Native Question" and British solicitude for the non-white population was at the root of both U.D.I.'s.[5] Nothing has happened since in Africa, however, to persuade the Rhodesians that European or Asian minorities could live safely and prosper under African majority rule. They believe themselves to be defending civilisation against anarchy and holding back at the Zambesi the threat of Communism.

Many of the "freedom fighters" infiltrated across the river into Rhodesia are trained in Tanzania, that nominally united republic which is supposed to include Zanzibar.

Twenty miles off the Tanganyika coast, the islands of Zanzibar and Pemba mark the meeting point of Arabic and African cultures. Zanzibari nationalism was the creation of the dominant Arab minority, although its Zanzibar Nationalist Party had some non-Arab support. In 1957 the Afro-Shirazi Party also demanded independence, appealing to the African three-quarters of the population. Six weeks after Britain granted independence in 1963 the Sultanate was overthrown by a *coup d'état*, organised from the mainland with advice and assistance from Moscow, Peking and Havana. The mutiny against President Nyerere followed and was put down with the help of the British, although they declined the simple military operation of rescuing the Sultan of Zanzibar from deposition and his

[5] The Declaration of Independence of 4.7.1776 accused the King of endeavouring to bring "on the inhabitants of our frontiers, the merciless Indian Savages" and, in asserting that "all men are created equal", said nothing about Negro slavery. Yet Labour Ministers in Britain insisted that the American "U.D.I." was different, being "for freedom".

subjects from slaughter. A Revolutionary Council now ruled the islands by terror and torture, flogging and forced labour. The first state to recognise the new régime was the Chinese People's Republic. Chinese, Russians and East Germans moved into what was now a Communist enclave within the Commonwealth. Cuba and Zanzibar exemplify the Communist method of using islands for the penetration of continents. "When you play the flute at Zanzibar", the Swahili saying runs, "all Africa as far as the Lakes dances".

In Rhodesia the Asian and the African were in paradise compared with the hell of Zanzibar. No Rhodesian Asian has pleaded, like his brethren in Kenya, to be allowed to emigrate to Britain. Despite drought and sanctions, there was little hunger in Rhodesia when Biafra starved.

It was on the morrow of the Commonwealth Conference at Lagos, where Mr. Wilson made his rash boast of an end to the Rhodesian rebellion, that the host Prime Minister, Alhaji Sir Abubakar Tafawa Balewa, was horribly murdered. The independent Federation of Nigeria was considered a showpiece of British decolonisation; but corruption, faction and the artificality of a union of three disparate elements, Ibos in the East, Yorubas in the West and the Hausa-Fulanis in the North, numbering about as many as the first two put together, made a military take-over almost inevitable, as in so many other new states.

Lugard had united Northern and Southern Provinces for administrative convenience. In 1920 the Northern Governor, Sir Hugh Clifford, described the idea of Nigerian nationhood as farcical. Politicians and intellectuals like Dr. Azikiwe nourished the ideal of one nation. Many of the early nationalists however thought of themselves as West Africans and, when their hopes of wider federation were dashed, tribal loyalties reasserted themselves.

105

Separatism was no Ibo monopoly. Both Northern Emirs and Yorubas of the West threatened secession in 1951 and 1953 respectively. In those days the Northern People's Congress led by the Sardauna of Sokoto preferred a loose confederacy. That was before oil was struck in the East.

The Sardauna, who was Premier of the Northern Region, perished in the same *coup* as his "lieutenant" in Lagos, Sir Abubakar. It was the work of young officers, mainly Ibo. General Ironsi, the Ibo who was made Federal Military Governor and Supreme Commander, had himself been marked for arrest. So had Lieutenant-Colonel Ojukwu, son of one of the richest men in Nigeria.

Unequal to his task and pushed by Ibo and Yoruba reformers, Ironsi announced in May, 1966 the abolition of the three Regions and their merger in a unitary republic. Ibo firebrands in the North acclaimed Ironsi as an Ibo, rather than a Nigerian, leader. A "pogrom" ensued. The word is apposite. Ibos were disliked, as Jews have been disliked, for their intelligence, energy and success. They differed, in faith and character and in their educational lead over a conservatively Islamic North, in their more egalitarian tradition of decisions taken through Councils of Elders, rather as the Christian and pagan Southern Sudanese differed from their northern overlords. In July Northern soldiers arrested and killed Ironsi and the Chief of Staff of the Nigerian Army, Lieutenant-Colonel Gowon, emerged as head of yet another revolutionary régime.

In September, 1966 both East and North proposed a looser association of Regions. The massacres were extended from Ibos to other Easterners, Efiks, Ibibios and Ijaws. Estimates of the dead vary from 10,000 to 30,000. More than a million Ibos escaped to the East, leaving behind burnt and looted homes and shops. Reprisals were taken

106

against Hausas in Enugu, Onitsha, Port Harcourt and other Eastern towns. The survivors were repatriated. A meeting between the General and the Colonel at Aburi, in Ghana, was abortive.

On the 30th May, 1967, Ojukwu proclaimed the Republic of Biafra. On July 6th Federal troops entered his territory, under orders from General Gowon to "penetrate into the East Central State and capture Ojukwu and his rebel gang".

It took British arms, Soviet guns and aircraft and Egyptian pilots to enable the Federal forces to subdue the secessionists. It took until January, 1970. Soviet influence in Nigeria has increased as a result of a conflict in which Portugal and South Africa, Zambia and Tanzania found themselves backing Biafra while Britain, the U.S.S.R. and the U.A.R. were supporting General Gowon.[6]

Commonwealth Africa was divided; likewise the *francophone* states. The sentiments of ordinary people did not necessarily follow their government's lead. The struggle in the South Sudan seldom makes even a headline. The Nigerian war was seldom absent from the press and radio and television of the world. Passions were aroused, parties divided as over Spain, Munich and Suez. About two million people died, which is something like twice the Congo toll of death. In a sense they perished in perpetuation of imperial frontiers. Ironically, that is the only legitimacy in post-colonial Africa. Africa must not be "balkanised". That is an article in the creed of the Organisation of African Unity. Like Europe in the Dark Ages the successors cling to the legacy of Caesar. Katangese, Biafrans or Southern Sudanese have been taught a lesson in blood that the ex-

[6] The Portuguese attitude was essentially one of common humanity. Facilities were provided at São Tomé for airlifts to Biafra of food and medical supplies.

107

alted principle of self-determination, enshrined in the United Nations Charter, does not apply to them and is to be selectively interpreted. The cynical reflect moreover that where oil gushes blood flows.

Félix Houphouet-Boigny observed in May, 1968:

> "If we all are in agreement in the O.A.U. in recognising the imperious necessity of unity, unity as the ideal framework for the full development of the African man, we cannot admit for ourselves that it should become his grave."

The President of the Ivory Coast recalled that Mali and Senegal had separated and met "again within a regional grouping". The insistent question remains: to what extent can unity be constructed against the tribal realities of post-colonial Africa?

The sub-plot in the Biafran tragedy was the rivalry and intrigues of European interests and governments, particularly France and Britain upon whom the unity of Europe and the stability of the two interdependent continents largely depend. One day we shall learn the truth.

Many Ibos have sought work in what was Spanish Guinea. Disciplined toil has little appeal for the Fangs of its mainland part, Rio Muni, or the Bubis of the island of Fernando Pó. The horrors in the Ibo homeland obscured the "mini-Congo" in this territory which in October, 1968, after 190 years of Spanish rule, received the blessings of independence. In the Congo, mutiny in the *Force Publique* was the first plunge into chaos. In Equatorial Guinea, as it was now styled, trouble started in February, 1969, with dissension over 250 Civil Guards left behind under treaty. The local Spaniards smelt the heavy air and began to decamp. The Foreign Minister and others vainly attempted a *coup*. As in the Congo, the former metropolitan power came back to the rescue of an economy in collapse. Spain had only produced in her Guiné 35 graduates, five lawyers and two agronomists, from a population of 255,000.

European retreat and Soviet advance! Some thought it strange that General Franco's government should have granted Russia a fishing base in the Canaries. As Mauritius, who has done likewise, is nervously aware, Soviet fishing fleets are part of an intelligence system. Lines of Soviet ambition ran from North Africa to the West Coast and extended across the Atlantic to Cuba. The Russians built Nkrumah an air base at Tamale which far exceeded Ghana's requirements.[7] The U.S.S.R. and U.A.R. took advantage of the Nigerian struggle. Soviet guns and Egyptian-piloted MIG's were no disinterested tribute to the legitimacy of General Gowon.

Cuba had its "Gulf of Guinea subversion plan", which was disclosed to the West by the defecting diplomat, Dr. Leonel Alonso. Fidel Castro has high regard for Amílcar Cabral, who attended the Tricontinental Congress and provides him with technicians, radio operators and doctors. Cuban officers have served against the Portuguese who defend the only territory in West Africa north of the Equator in the possession of a N.A.T.O. power.[8]

Two hundred and seventy-six miles out to sea lie the Cape Verde Islands. Amílcar Cabral is half Cape Verdian. The Portuguese province of Guiné was formerly administered with the islands and the Cape Verdians are an *élite* within the province and within P.A.I.G.C. which is short for African Party for the Independence of Guiné-Bissau and Cape Verde. The liberation of the islands—"liberation"

[7] The Yugoslavs built the Ghanaian naval base of Sekondi, near Takoradi.

[8] See the author's *Portuguese Guinea: Nailing a Lie* (Congo-Africa Publications, 2 Old Burlington Street, London, S.W.1, 1970). Cuba has also sent instructors to Congo-Kinshasa, Congo-Brazzaville and Tanzania.

is an odd expression since they were uninhabited[9] when the Portuguese settled them—has been described by Amílcar Cabral as "indispensable to the freedom struggle of Angola, Mozambique and South Africa". He wrongly terms the all-weather airport in the island of Sal "South African". Certainly a loan from South Africa has been negotiated to improve it, and the erection of the Arab-African air barrier against the West which, since the fall of King Idris in 1969, has encompassed Libya, has made Sal an important stage on the Cape route and an objective of those who would cut the lifelines of Europe. Sal also houses the British and other staff serving the submarine cable from the Cape through Lisbon to London.

Those lifelines are beset by Soviet submarines. The Red Fleet shows the Red Flag in all the seas round Africa. Apart from France's Djibouti, the only African bases, or "facilities", to use the post-colonial expression—"bases" are imperialistic!—upon which the West could count in war are either South African or Portuguese. The terrorist operation against Southern Africa have so far been beaten back. They have no roots in the masses. Mao compared guerrilla fighters with "fish" swimming freely in the "water" which denotes the people to be "liberated". In Portuguese Africa, Rhodesia, South Africa and South-West Africa they have been fish out of water. Sekou Touré gave the game away when he spoke of the liberation of those who did not want to be liberated.

[9] In 1964 the Soviet delegate denounced brutal British oppression of the indigenous inhabitants of Mauritius, the Seychelles and St. Helena. Mr. C. D. King replied for Britain that it was "even worse than the Soviet delegate realised". "The indigenous inhabitants of Mauritius were all speedily liquidated. They were dodo which being extinct, could not claim independence on the basis of one bird, one vote." The original inhabitants of Seychelles were giant tortoises, of St. Helena, various birds.

In the future however Russian maritime forces could be used in African waters as they have been in the Mediterranean, to "show the flag" in stimulation of guerrilla operations. The ships, aircraft and naval infantry of the Soviet Union may give more potent reinforcement to those they call "freedom fighters" than any they have so far received from the United Nations, the Organisation of African Unity and the World Council of Churches.

The Communist Party of South Africa is the oldest in the continent, having been founded in 1921.[10] In 1966 the *Wall Street Journal* reported an interview with the South African Communist leader, Braam Fischer. Why, he was asked, was his party "so especially keen on overthrowing South Africa? Was it the gold mines?" He replied : "I will trade you all the gold mines in South Africa for Cape Point." That single sentence links the subversive struggle in Southern Africa with the capture of strategic objectives for major conflict.

The Cape is the crossroads of the only all weather deep sea route connecting the Atlantic seaboards of America, Europe and Africa with the Indian Ocean and Pacific shores of Africa, Asia and Australasia. Ice bars the northern coasts of Canada for much of the year; Cape Horn is a hazard. If Suez can be blocked, so can Panama. The Cape of Good Hope, under present auspices, is open to shipping in all seasons. It is indeed our "good hope".

---

[10] The Party's influence declined when Moscow began to demand that it work for a black republic.

Chapter XII

Co-existence and Co-operation

The generalisations of inferior journalism reduce the African situation to the confrontation of white *versus* black —even the pigmentation is oversimplified; black North *versus* a white South, which includes the multi-racial Portuguese and several Black states; colonialism in the south and neo-colonialism in the north, *versus* African nationalism and African unity.

African unity is even less of a fact than Arab unity. What is African nationalism? The Imperialist powers in retreat and their African adversaries took their cue from Asia. But from neither point of view was Asia a true comparison. Because Asian dependencies appeared ripe for a transfer of power to indigenous hands, it did not follow that the African colonies were ready for independence. Whereas in India, Indo-China and Indonesia, those who contended for independence could evoke a past of high civilisation and organised polity, the ancient glories of Africa were not a matter of memory or of recent history, but of antiquarian and nationalistic reconstruction. Nigeria, for example, became a part of the British Empire and then a sovereign independent member of the Commonwealth within a single lifetime. Similarly, there were aged Burmese who had witnessed the annexation of their country to the Indian Empire and were still alive when it became an independent republic outside the Commonwealth. But what was restored in Burma had never existed in Nigeria, whose tribes and emirates had not constituted even "a geographi-

112

cal expression". The Indo-Pakistan sub-continent had never experienced a complete political unity but its pre-European empires had dealt with the European powers on equal terms and sometimes from positions of superiority.

There were Indian and Burmese nationalist movements. There was no African nationalist movement. There were tribal Africans and Africans who had learnt to think of themselves as Portuguese or French. British Imperialism exerted less pressure to impose cultural assimilation, but British Africans learnt to call themselves, however, half-heartedly, Nigerians or Kenyans. African nationalism was a series of movements, each of which accepted and agitated within the frontiers of the "scramble". Each expressed the yearning and asserted the demands, particularly of an *élite* for respect, equality, status and power. However, in Africa the historical basis on which to base a claim for political independence was little more than a memory of slavers, conquest and annexation.

Sir Abubakar Tafawa Balewa, the murdered Prime Minister of Federal Nigeria, speaking of the haphazard and artificial boundaries of colonialist convenience "which often cut right across even the former groupings", went on to say that "however artificial boundaries were at first, the countries they created have come to regard themselves as units, independent of one another". As such, they sought admission to the U.N. "It is therefore our policy to leave these boundaries as they are at present and to discourage any adjustment whatever."

To revise frontiers was too dangerous. African leaders did not wish to admit its paradoxes. Re-demarcation would endanger the larger ideal of Pan-African brotherhood and African unity, which in fact emerged from the Pan-Negroism that began with West Indian and American

H 113

Negroes such as James and Du Bois. Nkrumah's Accra conference of 1958 registered the transfer of Pan-Negro ideas to those of a continentalism which reflected his own ambitions and those of the East, rather than logic or reality. Nkrumah continued to sympathise with the Negroes of the Americas and said as much when he visited Haarlem, but his political outlook was continentalist. This meant that the Egyptians were Africans, even if the Portuguese and Afrikaners were not. Nasser gave his assent to this interpretation in *The Philosophy of the Revolution* :

". . . we cannot, in any way, stand aside even if we wish to, from the sanguinary and dreadful struggle now raging in the heart of the continent between five million whites and two hundred million Africans. We cannot do so for one principle and clear reason; we ourselves are in Africa."

Just as world government has been the creed of would-be world conquerors and super-powers, so Pan-Arabism and Pan-Africanism have been the expression of continental expansionists. Chief Awolowo never made any bones about "the United Arab Republic, the creature of Nasser, which has one foot in Africa and another in the Middle East . . . the very antithesis of a workable African community". After attempts at union with Syria and Yemen, the U.A.R. has turned to Sudan and Libya. During his State visit to Moscow in November, 1969 President Numeiry convinced Premier Kosygin of Sudan's potential for furthering revolution to the north, south and south-east.

Africa has witnessed the exile of Nkrumah to a villa in Conakry and the passing of Nasser from a country reduced to what Marxists call a "military semi-colony" of Soviet Russia. Africa has known :

"no Mazzini; no Gandhi or Sun Yat-Sen. This is not surprising. African nationalism differs from the nationalisms

114

of India or China in that Africa exists as an idea only, projected into the future, not as an historic fact. There has been no single comprehensive civilisation, no common background of written culture to which nationalists could refer."[1]

So history is remade, as it is in the countries of the Communist *bloc*, and facts denied. The Middle East and the *Maghreb* are miscalled an Arab world in which Berbers, Druzes and Kurds are incidental sojourners and the Jews a running sore. A racialist Monroe Doctrine is applied to Africa, so that the Portuguese, who have been African for five hundred years, and the Afrikaners, who anticipated the Bantu empire-builders three hundred years ago, and whose very name proclaims their tenacious commitment to the continent, are denounced as colonialist intruders.

But the Jew and the European provide for both these intersecting "worlds" that common enemy which is the only potent source of unity. The colonialists of Zionist *Aliyah* have come under the same "liberal" fire as the settlers of Southern Africa. The Afrikaner, in particular, shares with the Israeli a deep sense of destiny, of a divine call to a great work : the Bible is their common heritage. Jew and Boer wandered in the wilderness. They have reached their Promised Land and will not give it up.[2] Like his friend Churchill, Smuts saw in Zionism an ally of Empire, where Mediterranean and Middle East met in Africa and Africa joins Asia and Europe. South African Jewry has given *Eretz Israel* sons and wealth. South Africa's Middle East trade is largely with Israel. Both countries man outposts against guerrilla fighters, armed and indoctrinated

---

[1] Hodgkin, Thomas: *Nationalism in Colonial Africa*, 1956.
[2] At the 1970 census, next to the Zulu (3,930,000) and the Xhosa (3,907,000), the white nation (3,379,000) were the largest population group in the Republic. There were 1,996,000 million Coloured, who are closer to the Whites than other groups, and 614,000 Asiatics.

by Communism. Both countries are the target of Communist propaganda. Both have known Western arms embargoes.

In the past, ethnic exclusiveness has been a condition of Boer and Israeli survival. In the State of Israel, Nazareth is an Arab town, but beyond its ancient walls may be seen the aggressively modern homes of Jewish settlements. Tel-Aviv is Jewish; Jaffa is part of the same municipality, but it is Arab. Much development in Israel is necessarily separate. The Six Days' War gave the Israelis responsibilities for several "Arabistans".

Zionism is preposterously equated with Nazism by the extreme Left, and the parliamentary Republic of South Africa is caricatured as Vorster's *Reich*. But if Zionism and *apartheid* be racialist, racialist too are the forces that would "liberate" Palestine from the Jews and Southern Africa from the Whites.

The Communists, Russian, Chinese and indigenous, have suffered reverses in Africa. But they may well be satisfied with Western liberal and U.N. acceptance of Marxist-Leninist criteria and definition of such concepts as "liberation", "racialism", and "colonialism". "Colonialism" pertains to the disappearing empires of Europe and not to the expanionist empires of Eurasia. "Racialism" is inapplicable to Russia, that Nebuchadnezzar who has deported or exterminated millions of the racially undesirable, that Pharaoh who "will not let my people go". The *pogrom* is not an exclusively Tsarist institution. The victims of Stalinism and its imitators must exceed the entire population of the Republic of South Africa. Yet South Africa, in both King Street and Lambeth Palace, is rated not as a country where evil things are done, but as a uniquely evil country which should not be entrusted by its wartime allies with defensive weapons, still less permitted to continue to administer South-West Africa, which has been renamed "Namibia" and "taken over" by the U.N.

One of the earliest advocates of *apartheid* was Abraham Lincoln. He told Negroes, who after their emancipation visited him at the White House, that he thought it better that the white and the black in the United States should live separately. He proposed to settle Negroes in Guatemala.

In South Africa, the origins of *apartheid* go back to British colonial days. The Glen Grey Act of 1899 formalised the system of local self-government through native councils. The Transkei General Council was established in the following year.

There is a widespread misconception that separate development is a doctrine of fanatical post-Smutsian Afrikaner nationalism. Smuts may have seemed too "liberal" and lost elections in consequence, but in common with most South Africans, English-speaking no less than Afrikaans, he had no illusions about national democracy. In 1895, he said in Kimberley Town Hall :

"The theory of democracy as currently understood and practised in Europe and America is inapplicable to the coloured races of South Africa. You cannot safely apply to the barbarous and semi-barbarous natives the advanced political principles and practice of the foremost peoples of civilisation. Too often we make the mistake of looking upon democracy as a deduction from abstract principles, instead of regarding it rather as the outcome of practical politics."

About the time that the Union was born he said :

"I am against the policy of oppression. I would help the native in every legitimate way in accordance with his present requirements. But I cannot forget that civilisation has been built up in this country by the white race, that we are the guardians of liberty, justice, and all the elements of

117

progress in South Africa. The franchise is the last argument : more powerful than the sword or rifle; and the day we give away this final protection we possess we shall have to consider very carefully what we are doing."

In May, 1917 he told a joint meeting of the Imperial Institute and African Societies in London :

"We have realised that the political ideas which apply to our white civilisation largely do not apply to the administration of native affairs. And so a practice has grown up in South Africa of creating parallel institutions—giving the natives their own separate institutions on parallel lines with institutions for whites."

In 1923 therefore Smuts supported the Native Urban Areas Bill which provided separate living areas in cities for whites and non-whites. After recalling the increase in the non-white population and the surge of non-whites into the towns, he claimed that this had led to overcrowding, disease and crime, because of the unwholesome conditions under which native and white lived together.

"White civilisation in South Africa, which we should hold up, has been degraded by the conditions of the present system," he said. "The native on the other hand has suffered to an appalling extent as a result of this neglect. The native has come to our towns unprovided for—innocent, untutored people, who often fall into the hands of criminals and pick up diseases and vice." . . .

Even in 1929, when in opposition, Smuts returned to the same theme in his Rhodes Memorial Lectures at Oxford.

"If the bonds of native tribal cohesion and authority are dissolved, the African governments will everywhere sit with vast hordes of detribalised natives on their hands, for whom the traditional restraints and discipline of the chiefs and elders will have no force or effect.

"Urbanised natives living among the whites constitutes the real crux and it is a difficulty which goes far beyond the political issue [he said in the same series of lectures]. They raise a problem for the whole principle of segregation, as they claim to be civilised and Europeanised, and do not wish to be thrust back into the seclusion of their former tribal associations or to forgo their new place in the sun among the whites. . . . It is only when segregation breaks down, when the whole family migrates from the tribal home and out of the tribal jurisdiction to the white man's farm or the white man's town that the tribal bond is snapped, and the traditional system falls into decay. And it is this migration of the native family, of the females and children, to the farms and towns that should be prevented.

"At the same time I wish to point out that the prevention of this migration will be no easy task, even where ample funds are guaranteed to the natives. The whites like to have the families of their native servants with them. It means more contentment and less broken periods of labour, and it means more satisfied labourers."

"If Smuts, a man to whom the Liberal Party in England had been heroes, the man who had helped to create the League of Nations, the philosopher with the broad views of the human race, could reach these conclusions, who else in South Africa faced with the same responsibilities would have decided differently? Or if they *had* decided differently, even as far back as 1910, would they have had a chance of putting their views into practice?"[3]

As late as 1952, the Roman Catholic Bishops of the Union spoke of those "who have not yet reached a state of development that would justify their integration into a homogeneous society with the European".

Under later Prime Ministers, notably the late Dr. Verwoerd, the policy of separate or parallel development was prosecuted so energetically as to alarm not only the minority who, for whatever reason, preached the sacred doctrine of "one man, one vote", but those who believed

[3] Fisher, John: *The Afrikaners*, 1969.

in *baaskaap* and shrank from the loss of black labour and the other economic sacrifices which would be required. In 1960–61 Dr. Verwoerd proclaimed the removal of racial domination to be the essential condition of stability and prosperity. Each population group should control and govern itself along lines similar to the Commonwealth in an economic association with the Republic and with each other. There would be no federation but there might be a coming together as equals in a Commonwealth Conference of their own. None of the States would lord it over any other. They would live rather as good neighbours.

Dr. Verwoerd's successor, Mr. Vorster, announced that each state would be free to proceed to independence and to claim U.N. membership—as have Lesotho, Botswana and Swaziland.

In 1963, the Transkei, a well-watered area as big as Switzerland, became a self-governing Bantu state. Its constitution provides for a national Transkei citizenship, the use of Xhosa as an official language in addition to Afrikaans and English, with *Lesotho* also authorised for certain purposes. The brown-white-green flag of the Transkei flies alongside the *Vierkleur* of the Republic. The State President exercises authority with the *Bunga*, a Legislative Assembly combining traditional chiefly and modern elective representation. Responsible government is in the hands of the Chief Minister, Kaiser Matanzima, and other Bantu Ministers, who are at present assisted—as in Malawi—by white civil servants. Legislative competence for such matters as foreign affairs and defence, internal security, posts and customs, and the railways, still rest with Pretoria, but the aim is sovereignty, and whites are restricted to enclaves in the Transkei as are the Bantu in the white areas of the Republic. The white man has no permanent right to own land or to carry on his business or even to vote without special approval. He may not deviate from main roads or enter Black settlements without a special permit. The white man is a guest or adviser, but master no longer.

Self-rule has also been instituted for Ovomboland (South West Africa), Ciskei, the Tswana and the South Sostho and, at the request of the Paramount Chief, Cyprian Bekuzulu, a Territorial Authority was established for the Zulu nation in 1970. South Africa's liberal critics should study the institutions in the Bantu homelands and also in South-West Africa of fully self-governing communities. The British should reflect upon their own unsolved and explosive racial problem. In America the Black Power movement stands for ethnic integrity through separate statehood. The late Bishop of Bloomfontein was not always in step with his brethren of the Catholic hierarchy, but he was surely right to assert that a "state composed of a number of national and racial groups, maintained in their separate and distinct identities by the state of which they form a part", would conform with Pope John's great encyclical *Pacem in Terris*. South African policy has advanced beyond a federal to a Commonwealth concept.

Those who have no answer to the besetting problem of the age should not attack such an experiment. Furthermore, the bitterest critics of *apartheid* can find no less repugnant alternatives. The point is well made by Mr. Jonathan Guinness in a Monday Club publication :

"For what would it entail? If all inhabitants of South Africa were given equal political rights, there would first be a short honeymoon period under Nobel prizewinning moderate Albert Luthuli during which a few streets would be named after progressive leader Mrs. Suzman, then there would be a period of fearful civil war, similar to that in the Congo,

121

which would destroy the entire South African economy, after which some latter-day Chaka would impose a tribal dictatorship, disguised as a Communist or Black Nationalist state. Short of this, the other possibilities might have been first what might be called the Wild West system after the genial and picturesque genocide of the American Indians in the last century. This did not happen not only because the Bantu proved comparatively tractable and employable, but also because of moral scruples. Secondly, more recently, the South Africans could have applied the Israeli system, which consists in bringing in enough of your own people and encouraging enough of the indigenous population to leave so as to ensure a numerical majority. The time when this would have been possible was after 1945, when millions of displaced persons were milling about Europe in United Nations camps with nowhere to go and their numbers were suddenly swelled by further millions of Germans expelled by Poland and Czechoslovakia from the Sudetenland and the new Polish territories. These people have now long since been settled in West Germany, Western Europe, Israel and other places, but in the late forties Dr. Malan, then South African Prime Minister, could have brought in literally millions to the applause and relief of all the Western allies. The gratuitous expulsion, to make way for them, of millions of Bantu would, however, by any sensible standards have been a worse crime than the retention of those Bantu subject to the present restrictions on them."[4]

The affronts to human dignity which are part of daily life in the white areas of the Republic, and in many other parts of the world, are indefensible, but the shortage of labour, which has already made inroads into job reservation, is already making change inevitable. So is the decency of South Africans themselves. Is it perhaps not significant that inter-racial football is now played at the University of Natal, with the approval of the authorities? Mr. Guin-

[4] Guinness, Hon. Jonathan: *Arms to South Africa: The Moral Issue*, Monday Club, April, 1971.

ness explains why it is that Communists, "of all ruling groups in the world get away with the greatest amount of inequality".

". . . they are the best at talking the language of equality. Similarly, one reason why the South Africans run into such mountains of abuse is that they—despite a régime which is by world, and especially by African standards, not inhumane—do not even pretend to treat everybody equally or provide equal opportunity, but admit to variations based on race. Worse, they do not—like the caste-ridden Indians —even pretend to be trying to change things, to be bringing their ideas up to date or into conformity with fashionable concepts. But what puts them, for so many people, beyond the pale is that they are not some primitive tribe or unregenerate remnant of a barbarous civilisation, but Europeans like ourselves who *ought to know better*. This, basically, is why even the sincere Left is so completely insensitive to accusations that they concentrate on the racial inequalities of South Africa while ignoring, for instance, the downright racial tyranny of Communist Zanzibar; it is a compound of a dim feeling of *noblesse oblige* which is basically racial— we whites must set a good example—with the cultural equivalent of the Catholic concept of invincible ignorance by which, some say, you are protected from damnation if you are too stupid to know the truth. Zanzibar party bosses who are not brought up to our standards may rape what Persian teenagers they like, but the whites of South Africa, who know what Western ideas are, may not without obloquy exclude anyone from a park bench."

The Republic is the only advanced technological country in the Eastern Hemisphere south of Italy, and it constitutes the military bastion and the economic power-house of the unwritten alliance and growing economic association of Southern Africa. Portugal practices a diametrically opposite racial policy in Angola and in Mozambique, while Rhodesia demonstrates a very British tendency to compromise. Social segregation has been part of Rhodesian society since British annexation, but a republican constitution brings the races together at the parliamentary apex. Southern Africa is thus a political medley of black, white and multi-racial territories. Its enemies however successfully stoke the fires of hostility by misrepresenting South African policy and falsely alleging that Rhodesia, and more absurdly, Portugal follow the same "racialist" course.

It will not therefore be surprising if, north of the Zambesi, where there are intelligent observers and objectivity is not unknown, varying attitudes are taken to Southern Africa. President Nyerere can declare "no compromise with *apartheid*", and the Lusaka Declaration, issued in April, 1968, after the fifth summit conference of East and Central African states, spurned any dialogue with the minority régimes in Southern Africa. At the same time, the Conferences' Manifesto on Southern Africa, directed at foreign and particularly Western European governments, urged "our brothers in the resistance movements to use peaceful methods of struggle even at the cost of some compromise on the timing of change". Fulminations at Commonwealth Conferences and at the U.N. are commonplace. Yet there is small disposition to give financial aid to the sacred cause of liberation. When the Organisation of African Unity was formed in 1963, its Liberation Committee of nine, set up in Dar-es-Salaam, was bedevilled by the effect upon the resistance movements of the Sino-Soviet split, and, although each of its members was supposed to contribute to its funds, the resources of the organisation were meagre.

Not that those concerned saw any contradiction between the activities of the Liberation Committee, and the Charter of the parent body, which unreservedly condemned subversive activities on the part of neighbouring states or any other

124

states. Double standards are a feature of international organisations, including the United Nations, to whose charter that of the O.A.U. did obeisance. The members of O.A.U. were among those who, in the U.N. General Assembly, adopted in 1965, a resolution which included these salutary but ineffective words :

". . . no state shall organise, assist, foment, finance, incite, or tolerate subversion, terrorism or armed activities directed towards the violent overthrow of the régime of another state, or interfere in civil strife in another state."

The preamble to this resolution reaffirmed the principle of non-intervention enshrined in the Charters of various regional organisations, including the League of Arab States and the O.A.U., and that Organisation's declaration on subversion, adopted at Accra at a meeting of heads of state and government.

Unlike Israel, no Southern African government has so far struck back. President Banda has, however, warned black Africa of consequences more serious than those of Israeli retaliation against the *fedayeen* and their allies. Amid the clamour, one hears voices of caution and also of co-operation, the most outspoken and courageous being that of the *Kamuzu* himself. The President was a prisoner in Gwelo Jail during the "Year of Africa", but he has kept British District Commissioners in key parts of Malawi, besides the Secretariat men whose names appear almost too ostentatiously outside the neat bungalows in Zomba. Banda looks to Portugal for an outlet to the Indian Ocean at the great new port of Nacala.

President Banda welcomes South African aid and expertise. When the writer last met him in Malawi, he was welcomed jovially as an erstwhile advocate of the Federation that the President destroyed.

"Please remember me to Lord Salisbury and Alan Lennox-Boyd!" The President went on to recall his own youthful experience of South Africa as one of the many Nyaras whose initiation into full manhood was marked by a spell of work on the Rand. Then, no white man would shake a black man by the hand. Now the South Africans receive his Ambassador. What had all the pious anti-*apartheid* resolutions achieved? Who was prepared to send troops to suppress *apartheid* by force?

"I think," he concluded, "my way is better."

In Ghana that very intellectual Prime Minister, Dr. Kofi Busia, addressed his own National Assembly in similar terms. Thus in December, 1970 :

"What has so far been done to train and equip freedom fighters is woefully and hopelessly inadequate for them to wage a successful struggle against the well-trained and well-armed troops of the South African Government. Many of the members of the O.A.U. have either not paid their contributions or are heavily in arrears. At the last meeting of the O.A.U., I learned that only six out of forty-one members, including Ghana, had so far paid their contributions in full.

". . . However, if freedom fighting is to be persisted with . . . a re-appraisal of our attitude to it is called for. It would be necessary for members not only to pay the present contributions regularly, but also to consider seriously whether our clear intention is to arm freedom fighters efficiently and in adequate numbers to enable them to defeat South Africa in a full-scale war. The forces South Africa has built up are much larger and more powerfully-armed with sophisticated weapons we cannot match with our present forces.

"If war is our aim and chosen method, it should be clearly stated and demonstrated. Then the painfully ludicrous effort that has so far been made cannot escape anyone. If full-scale war is a clear intention then we must

126

be prepared to sacrifice commensurate proportions of our national incomes to build up armed forces sufficiently powerful and strong for the destruction of South Africa.

"We must make a realistic calculation of the cost in materials and in human lives of such a venture, and ask if this is the path to tread. What we appear to be doing so far is to send our African brothers to slaughter. I find it difficult as a human being and as an African to accept this situation without anxious questioning. . . .

"The greatest need in all independent African countries today is development. Our people need clean water to drink; they need adequate supplies of food; they need to be cared for when they are sick; they need good housing; they need education to equip them to participate effectively in the development of their respective countries. We are all engaged in the fight for prosperity and progress. All the resources available to us seem inadequate for these tasks, and we all look for outside help.

"That, as I understand it, is the reason why our efforts to equip freedom fighters have been inadequate. There are grim realities we cannot ignore. With the knowledge at our disposal, conscious too of the frustrations and persistent inadequacies of our policies of force and isolation, are we right in maintaining that the policies of violence and isolation are the only ones on which we must rely for ending the inhuman oppression in South Africa? Are we sure we can carry our peoples with us if we put this choice before them?

". . . We believe also that through dialogue, we could influence moderate white opinion in South Africa to seek an accord with the black majority for the purpose of changing the *apartheid* policies of the present régime of South Africa, or else of changing the reactionary régime itself by methods which only those who live in the country can legitimately use.

"We believe that without seeking such an approach, the moderate white forces in South Africa, in the face of threats alone from Africa, will be driven by fear and motives of self-preservation into the fold of the reactionary elements, because they will see a common danger in the policies of

127

violence and isolationism excluding any form of discussion. Anything, however small, that we can do to prevent such a solidarity of whites will help to hasten the day of the total emancipation of the blacks and the assumption of their full rights as citizens."

At the same time, President Houphouet-Boigny of the Ivory Coast offered to head a delegation to discuss with other African leaders the holding of a summit conference on South Africa and his foreign minister, M. Arsène Usher Assouan, told the ruling Democratic Party in Abidjan of the "duty to pursue a policy of contact and dialogue with South Africa". Support for this idea came from Gabon, Niger, Dahomey, Upper Volta and Togo. Dr. Busia commented approvingly that "dialogue . . . seems to me a more rational approach than a bloodbath".

What is South Africa's reaction to these approaches and how—to take the question a stage further—can she put her massive resources at the disposal of the impoverished states to the north of her? What has been the effect, so far, of her "outward" policy on the countries within her range of influence? To some extent, the process has been held up by Rhodesia's unilateral declaration of independence.

U.D.I. itself, the subsequent breakdown of both the *Tiger* and the *Fearless* talks, and finally the republican constitution, have kept the international spotlight on South Africa for five years, and since South Africa's "outward" policy demands delicate and discreet diplomacy, her northward overtures have been retarded. South Africa's and Portugal's refusal to apply sanctions have meant that, despite the Beira patrol, petrol can be cheaper in Salisbury, Rhodesia, than in Salisbury, Wiltshire. The *rand* has backed the "rebel" currency and South African police have collaborated with their Rhodesian colleagues in keeping the peace on the Zambesi. Black African extremism has taken advantage of defiance of the U.N. blockade to maintain diplomatic pressure against both republics, while the frustration of all attempts to subdue Rhodesia and punish her "accomplices" has helped to harden attitudes and sour the atmosphere of co-operation.

Nowhere has this been more apparent than in Zambia. Before independence in 1964, Dr. Kenneth Kaunda was talking in terms of exchanging ambassadors with South Africa.[5] Zambia is in many ways an appropriate objective for South Africa's "forward" diplomacy. The economic links forged by the mining giants of the Copper Belt, like Anglo-American—until recently there was a large community of South African miners working in the Belt—might have persuaded Zambia to look profitably southwards. It was ironic that U.D.I. which finally induced President Kaunda to curtail his ties with the south, necessitated additional trade with South Africa to fill the gap left by Rhodesia, so that, in 1968, South Africa, who, with Great Britain, is Zambia's principle supplier, sold her more than R.70 million worth of goods. Zambia's exports in return amounted to R.11,600,000.

But political animosity marred commercial expansion. Zambia placed a ban on visas for South Africans and her attempts to divert imports to Dar-es-Salaam from the south will prove more successful, if the projected Tan-Zam railway is ever completed, thus opening up Zambia to the trade of the Communist East at the expense of her Anglo-Rhodesian and South African suppliers. President Kaunda, indeed, is now more overtly militant than President Nyerere of Tanzania, who has already opened the door to Peking.

[5] As President, he engaged in clandestine correspondence with Mr. Vorster.

If Tanzania trains, Zambia stages, the freedom fighters, even allowing Africans from the South to be press-ganged into the forces of liberation, despite press outcry and public indignation.

Rhodesia, Mr. Harold Wilson, when Prime Minister, used to stress, was a British matter. It is then the United Kingdom which must face facts, and bear the odium of doing so. Once Rhodesia is recognised to be as independent as South Africa, it should be easier for the former links across the Zambesi, not all of which have been broken— Kariba still stands and the Rhodesian Railways still run— to be fully restored.

Yet, in spite of U.D.I., South Africa has extended her leadership and influence, and increased her trade with Black Africa at almost twice the rate of her exports elsewhere. Swaziland, Botswana and Lesotho have formed a Customs Union with their powerful neighbour. Indeed, their economies are interwoven with that of the Republic, so much so that the South African Wool Board makes no distinction between the domestic wool clip and that of Lesotho. Beef and slaughtered livestock from Swaziland and Botswana are exported to South Africa under controlled marketing schemes, administered by the South African Livestock and Meat Industries Central Board. South Africa also has an agreement with Swaziland under which all the latter's butter, tobacco, wattle, citrus and cotton surpluses are bought or marketed by the appropriate South African control boards.

For the three black states, labour is an important export commodity. Indeed the remittances of her workers employed in South Africa amount to one and a half times the value of Lesotho's exports.

Moreover, South African-financed schemes, such as the *Oxbow* hydro-electric scheme and the reclamation of part of the Okavango swamps, will make a substantial contribution to the development of Lesotho and Botswana, as well as adding to the water supplies of South Africa herself. The inescapable collaboration of the three ex-High Commission Territories with the Republic, including the contribution made to the development of Lesotho by the Rembrandt Group, has aroused speculation in African countries hundreds of miles to the north which have no common borders with South Africa. Some of them are rich in natural resources; all are poor in expertise.

Malawi possesses few natural riches besides her talented, hard-working and friendly people, and she has deliberately encouraged South African investment, advice and assistance. It was shrewd of the South Africans to lend Malawi R.8 million for the construction of a new capital at Lilongwe, after Britain had refused the loan, on the grounds that such a development was nothing more than an uneconomic prestige project. Further South African capital has been made available to extend the railway link to Nacala. Five South African firms now operate freely in Malawi (Roberts Construction is the largest employer of labour), and the call of commerce combined with the desire to lure South African tourists to such beauty spots as Lake Malawi and the Nhika Game Reserve led Malawi to take part in the Rand Easter Show in 1970.

Individual South Africans have held positions of great influence in Malawi. The head of the Malawi Broadcasting Corporation was a South African; South African officials serve with the Department of Planning, the Malawi Development Corporation and other government agencies. Unlike the British officials, they are seconded from their own government which continues to pay their salaries, and they thus arouse less jealousy from the local educated class. One example is Mr. David van der Spuy, a former Director of Information at South Africa House in London, who has refashioned Malawi's Department of Information and is preparing a qualified Malawian to take his place. In 1970, Mr. van der Spuy was sent abroad in order to reorganise Malawi's information offices overseas. His tour included Taiwan, which, like Israel, plays a discreet but important part in the development of African States which have been prudent enough to withold recognition from Peking.

Malawi is becoming known as the "Switzerland of Africa", where African delegations can meet helpful South Africans, and see for themselves the fruits of partnership with the South, just as the South Africans can rid themselves of many illusions about the black North.

In all this, the personality of Hastings Banda has played a decisive part. Presidents Kaunda and Nyerere may think the less of him now, and extremists may insult him as an "Uncle Tom", but his reputation stands high with elder statesmen such as President Kenyatta of Kenya and President Tsiranana of the Malagasy Republic.

France has been selling ships and aircraft to South Africa and also building up, and exercising with, the infant Malagasy Navy. The French Indian Ocean squadron is based on the Comores. France—Madagascar—South Africa is a potent factor in the containment of Soviet subversion and maritime power; and her association with South Africa and membership of the O.C.A.M. have enabled Madagascar to play a constructive role in African councils. Cut off from the continent, she has never been drawn into Africa's quarrels and can thus be a powerful force for conciliation. In the Congo troubles, Madagascar took the role of mediator and she has courageously defended the idea of dialogue with South Africa at the O.A.U.

Even before Houphouet-Boigny's political initiative, the Ivory Coast was trading with South Africa and more recently, Liberia, Congo-Kinshasa and even the Left-wing Congo Brazzaville, have become her regular trading customers. President Senghor of Senegal has allowed South African scientists and historians to attend conventions in Dakar and three Gabonese doctors visited South Africa in 1969. One of them was the President's *chef de cabinet*.

Of the O.C.A.M.[6] countries, the Democratic Republic of the Congo has been using two South African mining companies to exploit copper deposits in the south-east of the country. President Mobutu is concentrating on economic development rather than the political demagogy which marred the Congo's early years of independence, and what is potentially the richest of black African countries may in the near future draw closer to the southern sources of technique and investment.

Nigeria, greatest of Britain's former West African possessions, is absorbed with the self-inflicted wounds of civil war. Although South Africans flew for a time with the Federal Air Force, the Republic's alleged sympathy with Biafra has probably delayed the opening of official contact with Lagos.

The East African Community[7] may appear uniformly hostile to Southern Africa—but Tanzania's revolutionary socialism should be distinguished from the Kenyan policy of private enterprise in partnership with government. Kenya's rulers mistrust Communism, whether it be that of

[6] O.C.A.M.: *vide*, p. 55.
[7] On Tanganyika's independence in 1961, the East African High Commission, which since 1947 had administered inter-territorial services of British East Africa, was reorganised as a Common Services Organisation. A treaty signed at Kampala in 1967 turned this into the East African Economic Community and Common Market with its headquarters at Arusha.

133

the Chinese over the border, or those stirring the pot of Somali irredentism. Several Kenyan Ministers were educated at Fort Hare and have little time for histrionics. President Kenyatta has held the question of supplying arms to South Africa to be a matter for the United Kingdom alone, and not for its Commonwealth partners. In Uganda General Amin is more concerned about the Soviet aircraft and arms used against the *Anya Nya* insurgents in South Sudan, described as another Biafra and "Russia's Vietnam".

Many of these realistic politicians are veterans of the struggle for independence. Their successors will be more aggressive and more radical men. But they too will need to absorb the lessons of Africa's balance of power. As the futility of guerrilla action against Southern Africa becomes more apparent, confrontation must give way to contact and contact must lead to co-operation. In this, Portugal in Africa is already making a special contribution.

Chapter XIII

Portugal Remains

Because men are greedy and sinful, because super-powers compete for mastery, because moreover Africa is rich in minerals and points of strategic vantage, Portugal, in recent years, has found herself in the same international pillory as the Republic of South Africa, which pursues an opposite racial policy, and the Republic of Rhodesia, which hovers uneasily between the two extremes of non-racialism and separate development.

All three countries are condemned almost unheard. The Secretary General of the United Nations, U Thant, has refused invitations to come and see for himself the conditions in Portuguese Africa. Yet, other international organisations have reported favourably on conditions in these territories. The World Health Organisation has praised Portugal for the efforts she has made to vanquish leprosy and sleeping sickness in her Guiné province; at the beginning of 1971 the W.H.O. expressed the view that São Tomé and Principe "possess one of the best and most efficient health networks in Africa"; Portugal was also given a clean bill by the International Labour Organisation after its investigation into allegations of forced labour.

Portugal's overseas policy is the product of her history. Though condemned for the crime of colonialism, almost as a matter of international routine, Portugal is not a colonial power as were Great Britain and France in Africa, or as is Russia in Soviet Asia. Unfortunately, colonialism is a flexible term. Usually it is defined to suit the needs of anti-colonial colonialists, whose terminology is accepted at face value by those Western liberals who lightly accept Marxist terms and criteria. It is true that after the Treaty of Berlin, the term "colony" was applied to the *Provincias Uttramarinas*; but a "colony" for Portugal was a *colonia* in the Roman sense—a settlement joined by common citizenship with the metropolitan mother-country, as are all overseas Portuguese subjects today. In 1933, the Salazar constitution declared the colonies to be Provinces of Portugal in equality with the metropolitan provinces.

Five hundred years of Portuguese tradition in Africa make a difference. They distinguish Portugal from the parvenu powers of the "Scramble for Africa". Arabs and Portuguese alike were colonising the East African coast before the arrival on the scene of the tribes who now inhabit Kenya. Before England was locked in the dynastic strife of the Wars of the Roses, the Portuguese were on the coast of Guiné. Many former British territories first knew their masters within the memory of old men still alive. The Portuguese presence in the Congo is centuries older than the Belgian or French and has survived as well as either the bloody onset of independence in the 1960s. With, or without the flag, the Portuguese remain part of their tropical, no less then of their Iberian, environment.

Portugal is not only a European, but also a Eurasian and a Eurafrican nation. According to the Brazilian sociologist, Gilberto Freire, the centuries of Moorish domination of the Iberian peninsular accustomed many of its Christian inhabitants to look up to the swarthier Arabs. The folk legend of the *Moura Encantada*, or enchanted Moorish princess, expressed the envy of the natives for dusky beauty. Portugal is Semitic no less than Nordic, Arab and Jewish as well as

Celtic and Latin. Besides the quest for slaves, spices and souls, might not the call of their nomadic ancestors have impelled the Portuguese to explore and emigrate? Did their Arabian and African origins make their life between the mountains and the Atlantic seem the more inhospitable and confined? "God," wrote António Vieira in the seventeenth century, "gave the Portuguese a small country as cradle but all the world as their grave."

The "burning lands" of Camões' epic poem *The Lusiads,* drew his countrymen far afield. Prince Henry the Navigator encouraged intermarriage with the Negro women of Guiné. The Portuguese linked the culture of Western Christendom with that of the tropics. A dearth of authentic Luso-tropical pictorial art—doubtless due in part to Arab-Islamic inhibitions on the score of idolatry—is more than made up for in the realm of architecture. The European church and fort, the Arab tile, the Moorish horse-shoe arch and the Chinese pagoda were to be reproduced across the world. A number of tropical languages are studded with Portuguese words; that spoken in the palace of the Oba of Benin, but not understood by the ordinary Bini people, is said to derive from Portuguese.

Thus, when Mokwugo Okoye writes of the African influence in Brazil, and quotes the words of Gilberto Freyere;

"It was as though the hot and oleous air of Africa were mitigating the harshness of canonic discipline, Visigothic law . . . it was Europe that governed, but Africa that ruled."

he would do better to ponder the fact that, without the Portuguese, the culture that he prizes might never have existed.

Prejudice against this unique nation and its overseas policy is nothing new. The forces of Liberalism and Social

K   137

Democracy in the Protestant North of Europe have long been suspicious of Latin civilisation and, in particular, of the authoritarian régimes of Lisbon and Madrid. But in the nineteenth century it was not Portuguese "colonisation" which excited censure, but the apparent lack of it. Portuguese corruption and sloth were contemptuously condemned by British imperialists, who applied to their conduct of international relations the Darwinianism of the survival of the fittest, and who saw in the decadence of Portugal an opportunity for clean-living Anglo-Saxons to take over the remains of Portugal's once proud empire.

In a comment on a Note of 1891, the third Marquess of Salisbury wrote that Portugal's position did not "fit her to fulfil her international duties". Lord Curzon had nothing but amused contempt for the Portuguese administration in Gõa. In 1966 the anti-aircraft guns at Beira airport pointed skywards, not on account of FRELIMO, but because of Mr. Harold Wilson. Did the belief then that the British Government intended to seize Beira to strike at rebellious Rhodesia owe something to memories of earlier memories of British attempts at aggrandisement? In 1890, British designs on Beira led to demands in Portugal for the total boycott of British goods.

Pious Victorian rectitude turned up its nose at the racial impurity of the Portuguese. They were second-class whites, as Curzon described them, incapable of developing their African inheritance. Those who fulminate against the Cabora-Bassa dam, which will provide water, power and a livelihood for Africans of all races, colours and creeds, now make the contrary charge. They also on occasion identify the Portuguese with a policy of racialism and white supremacy. But what is a "white" Portuguese?

Those who in Guiné, Angola and Mozambique, and in

138

the African islands of Portugal, have mingled with every colour and cross-breed in cathedral, cinema, church and club, know that such an accusation is the most fantastic that could be brought. There is no colour bar in school or swimming pool. In the armed forces, all servicemen have "mixed" quarters and messes. In Lourenço Marques the author has been served coffee by a white waiter—the owner of the café was black. He also remembers meeting a working party of European soldiers clearing bush for an airstrip in Guiné. The sergeant in charge was a Fula.

There are exceptions to the rule that the Portuguese are colour-blind. Amílcar Cabral, one of the leaders of revolutionary subversion directed against Guiné, is said to have suffered from a colour-conscious superior while he was serving as an agronomist in the administration of the province. Yet Amílcar Cabral is as culturally a Portuguese as was the Governor of Guiné a century and a quarter ago who withstood French and British territorial claims on his province. The latter claim was only ended in 1870, when President Ulysses S. Grant awarded Portugal sovereignty of the island of Bolama, where English merchants had squatted since 1792. This governor was Honório Pereira Barreto, a Negro of Cachéu, the oldest settlement in Portuguese Guinea.

Nevertheless, a northern exclusiveness has been felt in Mozambique, where South African and Rhodesian influence is strong—and they drive on the left of the road. Similar attitudes are taken by certain ethnic groups in Brazil, herself the original of the Luso-tropical theory.

The *Second Report of the United Nations Committee for the Study of the Situation in South Africa* (1954), quoted Gilberto Freyere's experience and conviction that non-European and "integrated" societies can preserve the

139

essential values of European culture. The Report continued :

> "It is clearly seen that the present tradition of Brazil is considerably older than the country's independence and represents an expression of the policy adopted by Portugal towards all its colonies, a policy which in Brazil was maintained and strengthened under the Empire and by the Republic."

Brazil's solution to the racial problem has influenced Angola as much as has continental Portugal. The Luso-Brazilian Community, now offering Portuguese citizenship to Brazilians, which became a fact with the revision of the constitution in 1970, is, as Dr. Salazar said, "in line with the reciprocal interests and tendencies of the modern world". It is assuredly in line with the requirements of a strategy for the southern oceans and the Southern Hemisphere.

Commander Teixeira de Mota writes[1] of the "informal, personal and direct relationships" which European and African Portuguese in Guiné prefer "to those of class and caste". He continues :

> "The whole history of Portugal overseas involves a constant intercourse of different races and civilisations and neither colour nor culture imposes economic or social barriers. Individuals really mean more to the Portuguese than racial or cultural purity . . . Portugal's own history is a continuous process of fusion of races and cultures."

When the *Manifesto on Southern Africa*, issued by the fifth summit conference of East and Central African States at Lusaka, was placed before the U.N. General Assembly in November, 1969 and used to condemn Portugal, the head of her delegation, Dr. Bonifacio de Miranda, had no

[1] *Guiné-Portuguese: Monographias des Territórios do Uttramar* (1954).

difficulty in endorsing "the belief" expressed in the document :

> "that all men are equal and have equal rights to human dignity and respect, regardless of colour, race, religion and sex. This belief is also ours; and has been ours from time immemorial. In fact, we claim to be the pioneers of this belief in the modern world. For it was the Portuguese navigators of the fifteenth and sixteenth centuries who first spread the ideal of human brotherhood throughout the world they discovered."

To remove, if that were possible, Portugal from Africa might suit the purposes of Communism or even, for a brief while, the purposes of her competitors in trade and finance. It might assuage the sense of guilt felt by those who ran before "the winds of change", fanning them into hurricane force, and making a spurious virtue of supposed necessity. Portugal for her part knows that default of duty to primitive people is not virtuous.

To destroy Portugal in Africa would be as preposterous as to attempt to eradicate her influence from the culture of modern Brazil, or to prevent the integration within the United States of Hawaii, most of whose inhabitants were of Japanese origin. Integration in Africa has further to go than in Brazil, where it is not totally accomplished either.

Since 1961, however, all inhabitants of Portuguese Africa have enjoyed legal and equal access to the rights and duties of citizenship. Besides having their local legislative and other councils, the Overseas Provinces are represented in the National Assembly and Corporative Chamber in Lisbon on like footing to the Provinces of the metropolitan country. In his speech of the 2nd December, 1970 to the National Assembly, the Prime Minister, Dr. Marcello Caetano, made "social mingling, always and everywhere" the corollary of "the legal equality of all Portuguese people".

"We shall not give up our policy of racial fraternity; we shall not renounce our intention to go on with the formation of multi-racial societies; we shall not allow any compromise on the maintenance of a sole statute for the Portuguese of whatever race or colour."

Dr. Marcello Caetano has moreover announced a further delegation of autonomy to the overseas provinces, together with increased representation for them at Lisbon. Though Portugal is not democratic in the liberal sense of the word, the rule of law prevails, whether in Algarve or Angola, Mozambique or Minho. Authoritarian the *Estado Novo* is —but never totalitarian.

Portugal has much to teach the world about what is held to be a most dangerous and intractable problem. Her unique experience and achievement cannot be thrown away and rejected to gratify those who denounce her as guilty of racialism, while practising it themselves. Rather should Portugal be allowed the time and understanding to enable her to show Africa an alternative to the self-determination of white or black supremacy, and to build new Brazils on the African shores of the Atlantic. Portuguese Africa should also be allowed the freedom, if she so wishes, to forge permanent and formal links with Metropolitan Portugal. Such a process was encouraged by the constitutional revision of 1970.

Gilberto Freyere has described the Portuguese as a Ulysses, restless with the restlessness of Moor and Jew, restless within his narrow Iberian confines. For this Ulysses;

"the tropics were mother lands, native lands, and strange lands to which he returned with very special rights—almost the rights of a tropical expatriate who has wandered in Europe, absorbing her qualities in his blood, being and culture, until Europe has also become intimately his."

142

Portugal's aim has been thus defined by Dr. Marcello Caetano :

"to replace the Africa of tribal strife, endemic hunger, ignorant, suffering humanity, fear, magic and spells by a new continent, which, without denying its positive moral and social values, can take its place in the civilised world of our day."

CHAPTER XIV

What Hope?

"In the first decades of independence an endemic series of *coups d'état*, as well as the frustration engendered by the failure of black African nationalism to take over southern Africa (first clearly demonstrated in the results of the Rhodesian confrontation), have prevented much political or economic advancement. Africa has been steadily balkanised, and such tragic conflicts as the bloody 15 years war (in effect an Arab-Negro struggle) between Sudan and the coalition of Uganda, the Central African Republic, Tchad and Ethiopia (during which the population of the southern Sudan was reduced by four-fifths) have reduced its influence on world affairs to nil. Only Morocco, Algeria, Tunisia and Libya have achieved stability, through their reintegration in the European sphere of influence."[1]

Such, according to Anthony Hartley and John Maddox might Africa become by 1990. George Orwell's *1984* made Africa an East-West cockpit. In 1962 René Dumont[2] feared widespread famine in the 1970s. Yet in 1919 that neglected exponent of geopolitics, Sir Halford Mackinder, wrote that :

"The Congo Forest alone, subdued to agriculture, would maintain some four hundred million souls if populated with the same density as Java. . . ."[3]

The wealth of the continent remains largely unexplored and certainly only partly exploited.

President Bourguiba of Tunisia has on occasion depre-

[1] "The World Power Balance", *Daily Telegraph Magazine*, 3.3.67.
[2] *L'Afrique est Mal Partie,* Editions du Seuil, 1962.
[3] *Democratic Ideals and Reality: A Study in the Politics of Reconstruction.*

cated the word-war of African leaders against colonialism and neo-colonialism. He bade them shed "leftist" complexes and begin to work for the welfare of their peoples by applying their energies to the utilisation of the natural and human resources within their control. A praiseworthy number of them have taken this course.

But, as Messrs. Harley and Maddox indicated in their imaginary projection, the *Maghreb* is not Africa. For four thousand years it has formed one bank of an inland sea, intimately related with the opposite shore. The Sahara is more of a divide and a barrier than is the Mediterranean, separating as it does white from black Africa, the Mediterranean world from the black "Balkans" to the southward. Southern Africa constituted for Mackinder another "Heartland". What the three zones of the continent have in common are the ideas and institutions introduced by European empire and reflected today in Commonwealth or Community and networks of commerce, communications, education and finance; and all three, together with Western Europe, are subject to the pressure and penetration of superpowers. One may say that the great common factor is Europe whose interests, strategy and settlements extend not only from Norway to North Africa but from the North Cape to Cape Point.

President Bourguiba's Foreign Minister, Mohammed Masmoudi, charges Europe with a "dangerous myopia"[4] in face of a dynamic Soviet policy in the Mediterranean, the "prudence" of the United States, whose fleet has lost its North African bases, and the designs of Peking with its ally in Albania. Another distinguished French African, President Houphouet-Boigny of the Ivory Coast, gave warning as early as 1959 that under-developed but over-populated

[4] *Preuves*, 4th quarter 1970.

China was drawn to under-developed and under-populated Africa.[5] Africa, he concluded, must be an extension *(prolongement)* not of Asia, but of Europe.

A decade later the project of a Tan-Zam Railway gave the Chinese their chance to prepare a "liberated area" for intensified operations against Southern Africa. Like the Russians, they make their mistakes. Unlike the Russians, they are not regarded as white colonialists. They will not be easily dislodged. For Western Europe, Southern Africa offers a way round the Arab-African air barrier and excellent docks and installations. As an economic hinterland, it has nuclear and oil potential and gold which, if re-priced and produced in larger quantity, could form the monetary foundation of a vast and prosperous single or preferential market.

The loss of access to these advantages to Western Europe would drive her into unacceptable dependence upon transatlantic supplies and deprive the Americas of outlying defences. European and American complicity in bans and boycotts against them are thus against Europe, against reason and are a betrayal of the West.

Writing in *Southern Africa* as long ago as the 11th September, 1964, Mr. Alan Gray castigated the "liberal sentimentality" on Africa :

"Mere fashion should not be allowed to obscure truth . . . lessons are today being driven home by events that stem directly from the rejection of reality in favour of liberal sentimentality. . . . The light-weight body of opinion that has been guilty of placing Africa in highly—vulnerable predicament . . . must surely give way to a more serious

[5] Africa, the second largest continent, occupies 20 per cent of the world's land area and contains more independent states (43) than any other continent. But it has only 9 per cent of the world's estimated population (3,030 millions) and 50 per cent only of Europe's. The density of Africa's population is 165 per cm. per square mile.

grasp of developments. . . . If it does not, Lenin's road to
the conquest of Europe through Africa will inevitably lie
ahead and it will be traversed by China and Russia at tre-
mendous speed. A Western policy of active interdiction will
only prove possible if Southern Africa remains intact as the
base and pivot of that policy. If the Republic of South
Africa and the Portuguese Provinces are not given the support they deserve it will not be possible to build any kind
of Western strategy in Africa. Already isolated to the East
by the Iron Curtain, Western Europe could soon find itself
isolated to the south by an Ebony Curtain running the
length of the African littoral on the Mediterranean, menac-
ing access to the Far East at one end and access to the
Atlantic at the other. In addition, the oil supplies of the
Middle East would be gravely threatened and Communist
expansion through the Asia Minor flank would develop to
link up with the southernmost Soviet land-mass on the
Black Sea. In this Communist grand strategy, Western
Europe would be isolated on all sides except the Atlantic
one. The Far East, including Japan, Australia and New
Zealand, would also be isolated except to the Pacific. . . .
At the centre of these great oceans would be North America
—highly vulnerable master of the oceans of the world—but
no longer able to effectively intervene in the continued
spread of the Communists by every means short of war (but
not excluding guerrilla war) through the decisive land masses
of the world."

In the third Africa of the South, Portuguese, Rhodesians
and South Africans have built another Europe. The Portuguese, as we have seen, were an Eurafrican nation before
the discovery of America. In Capetown the late Dag Ham-
marskjöld exclaimed: "But we are in Europe." General
of the Army André Beaufre described the Republic of South
Africa as the *Cap de L'Europe*:

"In the sense that Europe is a projection of Asia, so is South
Africa the European cap of the African Continent. The
common fate of these two projections throughout their

147

history has been to remain different from the continental mass, Asia or Africa, and to maintain an individual civilisation."[6]

On arriving to take up his post as Ambassador to the Court of St. James's in 1964, Dr. Carol de Wet reminded us that : "South Africa is truly a permanent part of Europe in Africa." Conversely, President Tshombe of Katanga called Paris "an African and European capital".

The industrial power of the old Europe and the new Europe of the south can furnish Africa with alternative sources of defence and development to those offered by the super-powers and the Communist Chinese—at a price. René Dumont believes that "the necessary European and world co-operation, combined with more effort on the part of the Africans, can . . . conquer underdevelopment in twenty years".

But even the more modest aim of preventing further deterioration demands that Southern Africa should play her special part. Earnest internationalists who argue for co-existence and more trade between East and West should argue also for co-existence between Africa north and Africa south of the Zambesi; and African leaders who solve ethnic problems by mass expulsion should be slower to condemn those who solve them by separation. Africa is not a continent of compromise. "Multi-racial" alternatives to the Portuguese and South African solutions have nowhere succeeded in giving justice to minorities. Tribalism is the dominant fact and the large white tribes in Southern Africa also have their roots and their rights.

At the same time, South Africa intends to secure them through a policy of parallel development which in time will surely change under the pressure of opinion, even more

[6] *Perspective*, April, 1968.

of economic needs, but which meanwhile deserves fair examination. Anyone who underestimates the idealism of its proponents is gravely mistaken.

Addressing, as its Chancellor, Stellenbosh University on the 23rd February, 1971, Mr. Vorster exhorted the students to decide for themselves between separation or integration. He had chosen separation but :

". . . there is one thing you must not do—you must not neglect a man's identity. No person, no matter what his race or his level of development, his background or his wealth deserves to be looked down on. He is a creation of God, just like you."

Every individual and group had the right to consider itself different. For the sake of a peaceful future each must have opportunity. "The time is past when the coloured man sat in the back of the bus."

South Africa's *de facto* ally, Portugal, gives the opposite answer to a question that perplexes so many people. Metropolitan Portugal is a small country, not rich. Yet the smaller countries of Europe have at times been her teacher. Switzerland started the Red Cross; the Scandinavians the *Ombudsman* who has been adapted even by the conservative constitutionalists of Britain; the Dutch have been leaders in the sphere of mental health. Portugal, for her part, has shown the world that different races can live together in harmony under one flag.

But whether there is integration or no, the interdependence of Europe with Africa is a cultural reality. Modern European painters like Picasso and Modigliani were profoundly influenced by primitive African art. Bantu artists in South Africa study European techniques and use modern materials. Bantu jazz follows Western trends, but draws on traditional music.

In 1953 British experts reporting on West Africa and the late Dr. Verwoerd, then Minister of Bantu Affairs, debating the Bantu Education Bill, were deploring educational systems that forced Africans into a European mould. The Education Conference held under U.N.E.S.C.O. auspices at Tananarive, in Malagasy, and attended by representatives of twenty-eight African states, called for the "discovery of the cultural heritage of Africa and bringing it to the youth in the secondary schools". As the present South African Minister of Bantu Administration, Mr. M. C. Botha, said in September, 1970, the inhabitants of African countries would no longer "blindly take over everything that is Western". The Minister quoted another U.N.E.S.C.O. conference on education, attended in Addis Ababa by representatives of thirty-nine African states : "African educational authorities should revise and reform the content of education . . . so as to take account of African environment. . . ."

On the other hand, African culture is more a ritual of collective life than an inheritance set forth in literature and written history. So the Portuguese allowed it less scope than the culture of India. There are however bright Islamic and African threads in the rich tapestry of the European inheritance which derives above all from the Mediterranean and is therefore partly African. In the past Africa gave Europe St. Augustine and in the future may have much to give. Senghor, exponent of *négritude*[7] based his African Socialism on "the seminal cultural values of both Africa and Europe".[8] The concept of *Eur-Afrique* (a reality in Portuguese territory) refutes racial animosity with spiritual con-

[7] "West Africa in Evolution."

[8] *Foreign Affairs*, January, 1961. At a meeting of Africa and Malagasy in 1969 the Pope spoke of "the precious and original constitution of *négritude*" and of its value to the Church.

sanguinity and is an aspect of cultural co-existence and fertilisation for two continents, which are destined to form the spinal column of that middle *bloc* which, though never neutralist in the face of Communist expansion, will in time provide a more stable balance of world power.

In April 1969 two enlightened statesmen, one from the Commonwealth, the other from the French-speaking Community, met in Malawi. At a State banquet in Blantyre in honour of President Philibert Tsiranana of Malagasy, Dr. Kamuzu Banda deplored the condemnation and ostracism of Rhodesia and South Africa. President Tsiranana replied:

"We must establish a dialogue by all possible means. To repay racism with racism is to encourage racism, but when black people assert themselves with dignity they will carry the day."

151

EPILOGUE

The publication of a book dealing with world affairs in an age of turmoil, and not least one devoted to Africa, is bound to be outpaced by events; and before these words appear Britain may be bound for a new European destination.

Some 176 million Africans are already involved in one way and another with the Community in which France plays, and Britain is expected to play, a major part. *Francophone* or Anglophone, or Portuguese-speaking, Africa and Europe cannot escape each other. They are geographically linked and bound by strategy and economic interest. European civilisation and languages are the common possession of African *élites*. The mutuality of European expertise and African resources makes dialogue and co-operation, not racialist revolution, the course of reason.

Indeed a mighty partnership is in the making for the safeguarding of two continents against the varieties of Communism. A middle bloc and stronghold of the Western way is in the logic of United States retreat. The dollar has declined, *Pax Americana* is in question. As Americans falter, Europeans including Europeans of the African Diaspora, must resume for their own safety, and even survival, responsibilities no less important because no longer colonial.

The secular struggle is prosecuted on more than one plane. Our enemies are always as ready to fill a spiritual vacuum as a vacuum of material power. Modern Europe maintains or aids Christian missions. She has also exported her heresies, her rationalism, her Jacobinism, her materialism, her Marxism. The witness of African Christians, in the Kenya of Mau-Mau or the Guinea of Sekou Touré puts to shame the Laodicean lukewarmness of Europe. The black African Hierachy is stauncher than their European brethren for Catholic faith and authority. Few Africans are unbelievers : Sekou Touré says so. Very few are Marxists.

But apart from the truths and errors she has transmitted, Europe has been the apostle of technology, that great god of the twentieth century.

"Technological civilisation and the phenomena it brings in its train (urbanisation for instance) break into and overthrow the old social cultures, separate profane culture from religious life and destroy a certain balance between the social and the religious dimensions of man."

Thus Père Jean Danielou, S.J., in his *l'Oraison Problème Politique*.[1] Using an ugly word for an ugly, destructive process, he describes the "desecralisation" suffered first in a West which has still not recovered from the shock. It now afflicts Africa. The collective existence of Muslim, Animist and other societies "impregnated with religious values . . . in which the very framework of living provided a constantly renewed contact with sacred things" could not survive in their traditional form "the irruption of technological civilisation".

Until recently, the study of the Koran was the foundation of the culture distilled at the University of Fez.

"Today, the culture which the Moroccan students want is the technological culture of the West."

This Father de Foucauld foresaw.

[1] Artheme Fayard, 1965.

Cash economy, hospitals and housing schemes, higher material standards of living, are no answer to the Communism of Moscow. The abstractions of 1774 or 1789 will not refute Sino-Cuban doctrines sprayed from the barrel of a gun. Only true religion drives out false. Europe still draws on the spiritual capital of eternal verities. But she must renew her vocation of defending the values necessary to her salvation. They were formerly part of her very existence and she communicated them to Africa and other continents.

Jacques Maritain is among those who have exposed the vanity of rebuilding Europe

> "on a vague transcendental materialism. Europe has all too many of these fanciful architects or these so-called realist technicians. What she lacks are saints. . . ."

Indeed, in fulfilling her duty to Africa, she might hearken to Amadou Hampate Ba, the saintly Muslim of Bamako:

> "Without God nothing will succeed in Africa."

154

APPENDIX I

MAJOR REFUGEE MOVEMENTS IN AFRICA 1960–1970
*(With acknowledgments to the Foundation for the Study of
Plural Societies)*

Country	Date	Details
SUDAN	1960–	Estimated 250,000 refugees from Sudan in various countries including; Uganda, 80,000–100,000; Central African Republic, 25,000 according to U.N. report in March 1967; 75,000 in Congo-Kinshasa according to 1969 report.
CONGO-KINSHASA	9–28.7.1960	34,484 refugees repatriated to Europe by air and 10,000 by sea.
GHANA	1959–1961	5,800 refugees, mostly Ewe tribesmen, fled to Togo to escape political persecution.
EGYPT	Dec. 1961	Members of the country's 40,000 strong Greek community began leaving Egypt at the rate of 500 a week after nationalisation of land.
RWANDA	Aug.-Sept. 1961	Several thousand Watutsis and other tribesmen fled Rwanda after Bahutu/Watutsi clashes; 6,000 reported refugees in Uganda by 28.9.1961, in 1962, Rwanda told U.N. there were about 50,000 refugees from Rwanda in Burundi, the Congo-Kinshasa, Uganda and Tanzania. According to "Keesing's Contemporary Archives", (18895), at independence in 1962 there were between 100,000 and 150,000 Watutsi refugees abroad, of whom

Country	Date	Details
		at least 40,000 were in Uganda, 30,000 in the Congo-Kinshasa, 40,000 in Burundi and "some thousands" in Tanzania. (Latter country had 8,000 in 1963.) In 1966, the U.N. High Commission for Refugees put the number of Rwandese refugees in Burundi at 52,000, in Uganda at 70,000, in Tanzania at 12,000 and in the Congo-Kinshasa at 25,000, in 1966, Burundi claimed to have 80,000 Watutsi refugees from Rwanda.
ANGOLA	1961	After terrorist attacks, 250,000 refugees fled to Congo-Kinshasa and 2,000 to Zambia. Most of them have returned.
ALGERIA	1955–1962	250,000 refugees fled to Morocco and Tunisia in consequence of the Algerian war. More than 200,000 were subsequently repatriated.
ALGERIA	1962	800,000 out of 1,000,000 Frenchmen left Algeria immediately before and immediately after independence.
CONGO-KINSHASA	Dec. 1962	6,000–8,000 refugees fled to Zambia from Katanga after U.N. intervention.
ETHIOPIA	1962	Several thousand Somali refugees fled from Ogaden Province to Somalia after outbreak of hostilities along Somali-Ethiopia border.
GABON	20.9.1962	About 2,500 Congolese expelled from Gabon after violent dispute between Gabon and Congo-Brazzaville.

Country	Date	Details
CONGO-BRAZZAVILLE	Sept. 1962	About 130 Dahomeyans expelled from Congo-Brazzaville after being caught up in a violent dispute between Congo-Brazzaville and Gabon.
CONGO-KINSHASA	Jan. 1963	About 2,000 Katangan gendarmes fled to Angola after U.N. action against Katanga.
NIGER	Dec. 1963	About 8,000 Dahomeyans in Niger returned to Dahomey after a territorial dispute between Dahomey and Niger over the River Niger island of Lété.
PORTUGUESE GUINEA	1963–	After terrorist attacks, 50,000 refugees fled to Senegal. Large numbers have since returned.
ZAMBIA	1964	About 12,000 adherents of the Lumpa Church, led by Alice Lenshina, fled to the Congo-Kinshasa. There are also Zambian refugees in Angola.
MOÇAMBIQUE	1964–	After terrorist attacks, 36,000 refugees fled to Tanzania and 5,000 to Zambia. Most have returned.
CONGO-KINSHASA	Sept. 1965	About 15,000 Congolese involved in Communist rebellion fled to Sudan, 6,000 to Central African Republic, 25,000 to Burundi, 6,000 to Tanzania, and 25,000 to Uganda.
NIGERIA	Jan. 1966	About 3,000 Nigerian refugees fled to Dahomey in wake of *coup*.
NIGERIA	Sept.-Oct. 1966	More than 300,000 Ibo refugees fled from Northern Nigeria to Eastern Nigeria in wake of a *pogrom* by the Hausas.

Country	Date	Details
CONGO-KINSHASA	Nov. 1967	About 2,500 refugees fled to Rwanda following collapse of mercenary revolt at Bukavu. Later repatriated.
KENYA	1967	10,000 Asians fled Kenya in 1967 following racial discrimination by the Kenyan government. Other figures: 1961, 2,529; 1962, 1,922; 1963, 1,675; 1964, 2,944; 1965, 1,769; 1966, 6,000. Several thousand more left in 1968. Numbers also left Tanzania and Uganda.
KENYA	1968	Several thousand Asians fled.
GHANA	Dec. 1969	60,000 refugees, mostly from Togo, Niger and Nigeria, ousted from Ghana in clampdown by Ghanaian authorities on foreigners working in Ghana.
EQUATORIAL GUINEA	Feb. 1969	Nearly 7,000 Whites fled after engineered anti-Spanish disturbances.
NIGERIA	1967–1969	Estimated 480,000 Biafran refugees in Nigeria by end of 1969 in consequence of Nigerian/Biafran war.

APPENDIX II

MAJOR TERRITORIAL DISPUTES BETWEEN INDEPENDENT AFRICAN COUNTRIES 1960–1970

Countries Involved	Nature of Dispute
MAURITANIA/ MOROCCO	Since 1957 Morocco had claimed that Mauritania was an integral part of Morocco. In 1969, after the Islamic Summit Conference in Rabat, Morocco abandoned her claim.
MOROCCO/SPANISH SAHARA	King Hassan of Morocco repeated claims to Spanish Sahara territory in 1961 after 11 oil technicians had been kidnapped on Spanish Sahara territory and taken across the border to Morocco, subsequently being returned by the Moroccan Government.
MOROCCO/CEUTA MELILLA	The Moroccan Government repeated claims in 1961 to the Spanish cities of Ceuta and Melilla. The cities were handed over to Morocco in 1969.
TUNISIA/(FRENCH) ALGERIA	In 1961, Tunisia pressed claims originally made in 1959 for a block of land in Algeria (then under French rule). Claims repeated when Algeria became independent. Talks on a settlement reportedly began in 1969.
SOMALIA/KENYA	Before and after Kenya's independence, Somalia demanded the incorporation of Kenya's Northern Frontier District, inhabited largely by Somalis, into Somalia. Dispute settled at O.A.U. Summit Conference in Kinshasa in 1967 and agreement subsequently ratified at Arusha, Tanzania, at meeting attended by heads of government of Kenya and Somalia.

159

Countries Involved	*Nature of Dispute*
SOMALIA/ETHIOPIA	In 1961, and subsequently, Somalia claimed Ogaden Province in Ethiopia, home of about 750,000 Somalis. Dispute settled in 1967.
SOMALIA/FRENCH TERRITORY OF THE AFAR AND ISSA	Somalia has consistently claimed that the Territory (previously French Somaliland) belongs to her.
ALGERIA/MOROCCO	Incidents occurred along Algerian/ Moroccan frontier in 1962 concerned mainly with disputes over the ownership of Zegdou, Saf-Saf and Tindouf. There were clashes between the Algerian and Moroccan armies at Tindouf and Figuig in 1963.
GABON/CONGO-BRAZZAVILLE	In 1962 a long standing border dispute between Gabon and Congo-Brazzaville erupted during a soccer match between the two countries.
NIGER/DAHOMEY	A simmering dispute between Niger and Dahomey over Lété Island in River Niger, forming a boundary between the two countries, erupted in 1963.
GHANA/UPPER VOLTA	Border dispute between Ghana and Upper Volta submitted to O.A.U., in 1964, when both sides agreed to demarcate their common frontier.
MALAWI/TANZANIA-ZAMBIA-MOÇAMBIQUE	In 1969, Malawi claimed that the whole of Lake Malawi as well as parts of Moçambique, Tanzania and Zambia territory rightfully belonged to her. Tanzania and Zambia immediately rejected the claim; Moçambique ignored it.

INDEX

161

163

DATE DUE